William Wordsworth

BLOOM'S MAJOR DRAMATISTS

Anton Chekhov
Henrik Ibsen
Arthur Miller
Eugene O'Neill
Shakespeare's Comedies
Shakespeare's Histories
Shakespeare's Romances
Shakespeare's Tragedies
George Bernard Shaw
Tennessee Williams

BLOOM'S MAJOR NOVELISTS

Jane Austen
The Brontës
Willa Cather
Charles Dickens
William Faulkner
F. Scott Fitzgerald
Nathaniel Hawthorne
Ernest Hemingway
Toni Morrison
John Steinbeck
Mark Twain
Alice Walker

BLOOM'S MAJOR SHORT STORY WRITERS

William Faulkner
F. Scott Fitzgerald
Ernest Hemingway
O. Henry
James Joyce
Herman Melville
Flannery O'Connor
Edgar Allan Poe
J. D. Salinger
John Steinbeck
Mark Twain
Eudora Welty

BLOOM'S MAJOR WORLD POETS

Geoffrey Chaucer
Emily Dickinson
John Donne
T. S. Eliot
Robert Frost
Langston Hughes
John Milton
Edgar Allan Poe
Shakespeare's Poems & Sonnets
Alfred, Lord Tennyson
Walt Whitman
William Wordsworth

BLOOM'S NOTES

The Adventures of Huckleberry Finn
Aeneid
The Age of Innocence
Animal Farm
The Autobiography of Malcolm X
The Awakening
Beloved
Beowulf
Billy Budd, Benito Cereno, & Bartleby the Scrivener
Brave New World
The Catcher in the Rye
Crime and Punishment
The Crucible

Death of a Salesman
A Farewell to Arms
Frankenstein
The Grapes of Wrath
Great Expectations
The Great Gatsby
Gulliver's Travels
Hamlet
Heart of Darkness & The Secret Sharer
Henry IV, Part One
I Know Why the Caged Bird Sings
Iliad
Inferno
Invisible Man
Jane Eyre
Julius Caesar

King Lear
Lord of the Flies
Macbeth
A Midsummer Night's Dream
Moby-Dick
Native Son
Nineteen Eighty-Four
Odyssey
Oedipus Plays
Of Mice and Men
The Old Man and the Sea
Othello
Paradise Lost
A Portrait of the Artist as a Young Man
The Portrait of a Lady

Pride and Prejudice
The Red Badge of Courage
Romeo and Juliet
The Scarlet Letter
Silas Marner
The Sound and the Fury
The Sun Also Rises
A Tale of Two Cities
Tess of the D'Urbervilles
Their Eyes Were Watching God
To Kill a Mockingbird
Uncle Tom's Cabin
Wuthering Heights

William Wordsworth

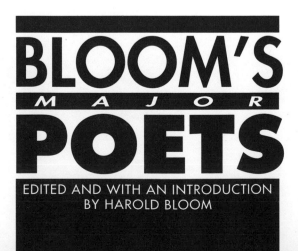

BLOOM'S

MAJOR

POETS

EDITED AND WITH AN INTRODUCTION
BY HAROLD BLOOM

3 5 7 9 8 6 4 2

Library of Congress Cataloging-in-Publication Data
William Wordsworth: comprehensive research and study guide /
edited and with an introduction by Harold Bloom.
p.   cm. – (Bloom's major poets)
Includes bibliographical references and index.
ISBN 0-7910-5114-5
Wordsworth, William, 1770-1850—Criticism and
Interpretation—Handbooks, manuals, etc.   2. Wordsworth, William,
1770—1850—Examinations—Study guides.   I. Bloom, Harold.
II. Series.
PR5888 .W454   1998
821'.7—dc21
98-37752
CIP

Chelsea House Publishers
1974 Sproul Road, Suite 400
Broomall, PA 19008-0914

Contributing Editor: Erica DaCosta

Contents

User's Guide   7

Editor's Note   8

Introduction   9

Biography of William Wordsworth   11

Thematic Analysis of "The Prelude"   15

Critical Views on "The Prelude"

    A. C. Bradley on the Originality of Wordsworth   20

    Lionel Trilling on the Sentiment of Being   21

    Geoffrey H. Hartman on the Romance of Nature   23

    Jonathan Wordsworth on the Two-Part *Prelude* of 1799   25

    M. H. Abrams on *The Prelude* and *The Recluse*   26

    Richard Onorato on Nature and "The Prelude"   28

    Thomas Weiskel on Wordsworth and Imagination   30

    Kenneth R. Johnston on "Home at Grasmere" in 1800   32

Thematic Analysis of "Tintern Abby" and the *Lyrical Ballads*   35

Critical Views on "Tintern Abby" and the *Lyrical Ballards*

    William Hazlitt on the Spirit of the Age   39

    Helen Darbishire on the *Lyrical Ballads* and Poems of 1807   40

    Robert Mayo on the Familiarity of the *Lyrical Ballads*   42

    Stephen Parrish on Wordsworth's Dramatic Monologue   44

    Harold Bloom on the Myth of Memory and Natural Man   45

    John Hollander on Wordsworth and the Music of Sound   47

    M. H. Abrams on Two Roads to Wordsworth   49

    John Mahoney on Poetic Plans with Coleridge   51

Thematic Analysis of "The Ruined Cottage"   53

Critical Views on "The Ruined Cottage"

    Samuel Coleridge on a Tribute to Wordsworth   56

    Thomas DeQuincy on a Tribute to Wordsworth   57

    A. N. Whitehead on the Revolt Against Abstractions   59

    Frederick A. Pottle on the Eye and the Object in Wordsworth's Poetry   60

    John Jones on the Baptized Imagination in Wordsworth   61

Neil Hertz on Wordsworth and the Tears of Adam   63
Jonathan Wordsworth on "The Ruined Cottage" as
    Tragic Narrative   65
Thomas McFarland on the Wordsworthian Rigidity   67

Works by William Wordsworth   69
Works about William Wordsworth   70
Index of Themes and Ideas   74

User's Guide

This volume is designed to present biographical, critical, and bibliographical information on the author's best-known or most important poems. Following Harold Bloom's editor's note and introduction is a detailed biography of the author, discussing major life events and important literary accomplishments. A thematic and structural analysis of each poem follows, tracing significant themes, patterns, and motifs in the work.

A selection of critical extracts, derived from previously published material from leading critics, analyzes aspects of each poem. The extracts consist of statements from the author, if available, early reviews of the work, and later evaluations up to the present. A bibliography of the author's writings (including a complete list of all books written, cowritten, edited, and translated), a list of additional books and articles on the author and the work, and an index of themes and ideas in the author's writings conclude the volume.

~

Harold Bloom is Sterling Professor of the Humanities at Yale University and Henry W. and Albert A. Berg Professor of English at the New York University Graduate School. He is the author of over 20 books and the editor of more than 30 anthologies of literary criticism.

Professor Bloom's works include *Shelley's Mythmaking* (1959), *The Visionary Company* (1961), *Blake's Apocalypse* (1963), *Yeats* (1970), *A Map of Misreading* (1975), *Kabbalah and Criticism* (1975), and *Agon: Toward a Theory of Revisionism* (1982). *The Anxiety of Influence* (1973) sets forth Professor Bloom's provocative theory of the literary relationships between the great writers and their predecessors. His most recent books include *The American Religion* (1992), *The Western Canon* (1994), *Omens of Millennium: The Gnosis of Angels, Dreams, and Resurrection* (1996), and *Shakespeare: The Invention of the Human* (1998).

Professor Bloom earned his Ph.D. from Yale University in 1955 and has served on the Yale faculty since then. He is a 1985 MacArthur Foundation Award recipient and served as the Charles Eliot Norton Professor of Poetry at Harvard University in 1987–88. He is currently the editor of other Chelsea House series in literary criticism, including BLOOM'S NOTES, BLOOM'S MAJOR SHORT STORY WRITERS, MAJOR LITERARY CHARACTERS, MODERN CRITICAL VIEWS, MODERN CRITICAL INTERPRETATIONS, and WOMEN WRITERS OF ENGLISH AND THEIR WORKS.

Editor's Note

My Introduction passionately defends Wordsworth against the covens of his current academic detractors of the Cultural Studies variety.

The Critical Views presented here, all two dozen of them, are so rich and valuable as to defy rapid summary. I therefore will comment upon only a few high points. A. C. Bradley begins the modern appreciation of the Sublime Wordsworth, as opposed to the Arnoldian Poet of Nature. This more transcendental Wordsworth is expounded by M. H. Abrams and Thomas Weiskel, in particular.

The great Romantic critic William Hazlitt sets the tone for the commentary upon the lyric Wordsworth, while the Romantic critics Coleridge and De Quincey begin the appreciation of the "Tale of Margaret" or *The Ruined Cottage*. The excerpt from Frederick A. Pottle is of particular insight and value.

Introduction

HAROLD BLOOM

After Shakespeare, Chaucer, and Milton, Wordsworth is the strongest poet in the English language. Shakespeare and Chaucer created men and women, which is the highest poetic achievement. Wordsworth, like Milton, is a poet of the Sublime, of the transcendental striving that is a vital part of the human endowment. Sir John Falstaff and Hamlet, the Wife of Bath and the Pardoner—these are beyond Milton and Wordsworth. Milton's Satan is an extraordinary creation, but he belongs to a different order of persuasiveness than Shakespeare's Iago represents. Wordsworth's Margaret, in *The Ruined Cottage*, is a figure of heroic pathos, but again this is in a different realm from the terrifying pathos of King Lear and Cordelia. This of course is to catalog the modes of greatness, and is intended to appreciate Wordsworth, since no other poet writing in English, after nearly two centuries, approaches Wordsworth's power and originality. "Originality" is the key term in apprehending Wordsworth; he made a larger break with literary tradition than anyone after him, be it Whitman, Dickinson, Eliot. After Wordsworth, poetry became Wordsworthian, which is still its condition as we approach millennium. Modern and post-Modernism alike are still in Wordsworth's shadow.

Before Wordsworth, poems had subjects; after Wordsworth, poems are subjective, even when they struggle not to be. The change, so commonplace that we now have difficulty in observing it, is the largest I know of in literature since Shakespeare's pragmatic invention of the human—that is to say, of the ever-growing inner self. No one before Wordsworth would have written a poem at all comparable to *The Prelude*, an epic whose principal concern is the growth of the poet's own mind. "Mind," for Wordsworth, was a very complex metaphor for consciousness, not just in the cognitive sense but also in the mode of affect. Wordsworth's best critics always have emphasized his uncanny fusion of the Sublime—"Something evermore about to be"—and of the educational mission of teaching us how to *feel*, more subtly and more acutely. The most profound function of Wordsworth's poetry is *consolation*, not through otherworldly hopes and speculations, but through the human heart and its universal struggle with the burden of mortality. No poet since Wordsworth can rival him in his power of evoking our deepest fears, longings, and anxieties of expectations. Wordsworth's cognitive originality, profound as it is, nevertheless is dwarfed by his emotional range and intensity.

We are at a bad moment, at least in the English-speaking world, in the study and appreciation of the greatest literature, whether it be Shakespeare or Wordsworth. An extraordinary number of those who now teach Wordsworth, and write about him, manifest their political and cultural exuberance in denouncing the poet of *The Prelude, Tintern Abbey,* and *The Ruined Cottage* because of his "betrayal" of the French Revolution. This peculiar fashion of academic abuse will pass away in a decade or so, while Wordsworth's greatest poetry will abide. To be one of the four most essential poets of the English language, is to be inescapable. Wordsworth will bury his historicist, Marxist, and pseudo-feminist undertakers. Even those who never have read Wordsworth are now overdetermined by him; you cannot write a poem in English without treading upon his ground. Doubtless all of us would prefer that Wordsworth had retained the generosity and social vision of his youth in his later years, but political objections are absurdly irrelevant to the perpetual greatness of *The Prelude, Tintern Abbey,* and *The Ruined Cottage.* If we reach the Twenty-second century, then Wordsworth will be there, undiminished and imaginatively powerful, a blessed consolation in our distress. ❀

Biography of
William Wordsworth

(1770–1850)

Born in Cockermouth in Cumberland, England, on April 7, 1770, William Wordsworth was the second of five children in a professional, middle-class family. His father, John Wordsworth, a lawyer employed by the powerful Sir James Lowther, looked after the Lowther interests, both financial and political. Like his own father, who had also been an agent for the Lowthers, John held an important position in the community; the Lowthers were a dominate force in Cumberland and neighboring Westmoreland, having been a significant presence for almost a thousand years.

When William was eight, his attentive mother, Ann, died. The five children were immediately split up. William was sent off with his older brother Richard to Hawkshead Grammar School, where he was allowed enormous freedom. His father was generally absent from his childhood after the death of his mother, and he roamed the surrounding Lake District at will while receiving a solid classical education at Hawkshead. In 1783, John Wordsworth died, leaving the five children orphaned and penniless. Although the Lowther family officially owed a great sum of money to John, they had no intention of paying it. A resulting lawsuit against the Lowthers was not settled for decades.

William soon went off to St. John's College, Cambridge. His relatives pressured him to go into law, but William did not prosper at Cambridge and he graduated without honors. In 1789 the French Revolution erupted and Wordsworth went off to join in the uprising, or at least witness it. Instead, he impregnated a woman by the name of Annette Vallon and scurried back to the Lake District, ostensibly to secure an income and return to her—but he never did. He went straight to London and became fervently involved in radical politics— the abolishment of the monarchy, the end of aristocracy, the disbanding of the Church. In 1793 his first published work appeared: *Descriptive Sketches* and *An Evening Walk.*

At this point, William was forced to consider how he would create an income for himself, as his relatives had given him up as a hopeless vagabond. A sickly acquaintance who lived in the Lake District became impressed with Wordsworth and his determination to dedicate his life to poetry, and so agreed to share his own income with William and leave him a legacy if he died. This man, Raisley Calvert, did die quickly and left William an adequate sum that enabled him, temporarily, to forget about money matters. William had been a good friend to Calvert, but he had also been very careful that everything worked out in his own best interest.

William went straight back to London and became a disciple of the philosopher William Godwin. He lived a very idealistic, bohemian life, encountering and engaging many of the most brilliant and radical minds of the moment. After several months of London life during which he met Samuel Taylor Coleridge, William got a chance to take a small country cottage for himself and his beloved sister, Dorothy, to live together as she had always dreamed. He and Dorothy moved to Racedown Lodge in Dorset, and a serious correspondence between William and Coleridge began.

Dorothy was devoted to William and his poetry. She became his muse, editor, and secretary. It wasn't long before Coleridge also devoted himself to William, whom he believed to be a genius. William, Dorothy, and Coleridge became inseparable—working together, traveling together, sharing friends, and enmeshing their two households almost completely.

After an extended tour of Germany with Coleridge, William and Dorothy moved to the Lake District, into a cottage in Grasmere. Coleridge and his companions returned from Germany somewhat after the Wordsworths and settled immediately next to them. This was a period of intense friendship and happy, youthful idealism. Coleridge, William, and Dorothy formed the core of a tightly knit group that included Mary and Sarah Hutchinson, childhood friends of the Wordsworths, and John Wordsworth, another Wordsworth sibling. This period also produced the most inspired poetry Wordsworth would write.

The closeness of William and Dorothy has been a constant source of speculation among scholars. For ten years neither seemingly had a single love interest. The letters they sent one another were suspiciously like love letters, and when William's wedding day finally did come, it was so difficult for Dorothy that she did not attend. It is possible that the brother and sister were lovers, but it cannot, thus far, be known.

Wordsworth married Mary Hutchinson, his own and Dorothy's childhood friend. The three lived happily together in a house full of activity and children, a home that was the focus of a small literary cosmos. They were, most of the time, a family of six or seven, with Mary's sister Sarah, Coleridge, and Coleridge's children taking up long-term residence with them. (Coleridge did not like his wife.) William and Mary then had five children; two died in early childhood.

During these years, Wordsworth's political sympathies were making a slow turn toward the right. He was becoming the responsible married man with household, wife, and children, and his attitude changed toward the young and impetuous. Many of Wordsworth's followers felt betrayed by his turn toward respectability, and Wordsworth himself wondered at the change brought by age in his immortality ode: "Whither is fled the visionary gleam? Where is it now, the glory and the dream?" Many people found him to be condescending and didactic.

Although he had acquired a new patron, Sir George Beaumont, Wordsworth's financial situation became perilous. He had had to move continually into larger houses to accommodate his ever-increasing household. With the assistance of Coleridge, he published his *Poems in Two Volumes* in 1807, but it did not make him much money. With his slovenly self-indulgence and his opium habit, Coleridge began to become a nuisance. A rift formed between them—primarily about small domestic matters—which would never completely mend. As the family moved into their final residence, Rydal Mount, William took a job. His expenses were mounting and the possibility of a fortune from his poetry had diminished. Strangely, it was the Lowther family to whom he appealed for a position, which he won and which supplied him with a large income, though he had to collect taxes to earn it.

William became totally involved in his domestic life—educating his children, landscaping his grounds, and improving the house itself. He did published *Peter Bell* in 1819 and a series of sonnets called the *River Duddon* in 1820, but he himself feared that his muse was gone. It was, however, the *River Duddon* sonnets, published at the age of fifty, which secured his fame and fortune forever. *The Ecclesiastical Sonnets* appeared in 1822 as well as a tour book of the Lake District.

In 1843, Wordsworth's close friend and one-time rival, Robert Southey, died. Southey had been the Poet Laureate of England and within ten days of his demise, Wordsworth was offered the title. At first he refused it, feeling too old to fulfill the responsibility of writing commemorative verses for the Queen. It wasn't long before he was persuaded to accept it, however, and after this honor he didn't write another line.

He died on April 23, 1850. Both Dorothy and Mary outlived him by several years, though Dorothy had become bedridden and delusional years before William's death. It became Mary's task, upon William's death, to publish the "poem of his own life," as he had called it, or "the poem to Coleridge." Mary gave it a title: *The Prelude*. This autobiographical poem had been in process for more than fifty years, and Wordsworth had decided very early in its creation that it would not be published during his own lifetime. ❀

[The definitive biography of Wordsworth is *Wordsworth: A Life* by Stephen Gill, published in 1989 by Clarendon Press, Oxford.]

Thematic Analysis of
"The Prelude"

Wordsworth's spiritual epic, *The Prelude*, is a poetic contemplation of the process of creation itself and the growth of an individual mind. It is a chronicle specifically of Wordsworth's own growth, and in doing this Wordsworth becomes the first modern poet and the beginning of an aesthetic revolution.

The autobiographical poem was composed over the course of a lifetime; Wordsworth knew from as early as 1804 that *The Prelude* should not be published while he was living. He asserted that it was "unprecedented in literary history that a man should talk so much about himself," and perhaps he was loathe to face the critical reception, as battered and abused as he had been by critics for most of his life.

The Prelude has a very complicated textual history that must be sorted out here first. Wordsworth worked on this poem for more than forty years. His first drafts date back to 1798, and the last large-scale revision ended in 1839. Seventeen major *Prelude* manuscripts survive in the Wordsworth Library at Grasmere. There are two principal drafts of the poem, the 1805 *Prelude* and the 1850 Prelude; someone who refers to *The Prelude* is citing one or the other of these two. However, a third version, the two-part *Prelude* of 1799, contains many treasures of its own and is studied for evidence of progression and change in the mind of Wordsworth even though it is not a primary text. The manuscripts of 1799 and 1805 both indicate that Wordsworth considered his work complete, but he continued to make revisions for another thirty-four years, creating the 1850 *Prelude*. He had originally thought of the poem as an end piece, and then as a preparatory poem for an epic philosophical work called *The Recluse,* which he never completed; thus, Wordsworth never gave *The Prelude* a title. His wife, Mary, supplied the title after his death.

At the age of twenty-eight, Wordsworth began writing the two-part 1799 *Prelude* while he was touring Germany with his sister, Dorothy, and his close friend Samuel Taylor Coleridge. Wordsworth and Coleridge had planned to write a great philosophical poem called *The Recluse* together, but it was not materializing. With *The Recluse* languishing, Wordsworth searched his past for reasons, and 1799 *Prelude* is the result. Part I is a reminiscence of childhood and an exploration of its formative powers. Part II is an account of his adolescence. The poem concludes in a valediction to Coleridge, who is present implicitly throughout the work.

Wordsworth decided to extend the poem and created the thirteen-book 1805 *Prelude*, considered now to be his greatest achievement and his best *Prelude*, but it was not always considered so. This poem takes Wordsworth through his years at Cambridge, his experiences in France and the French Revolution, his involvement with the philosopher Godwin, his spiritual breakdown in the spring of 1796, and his recovery through the experience of nature. It was during the writing of this 1805 *Prelude* that Wordsworth decided that the poem should not be published if it was not placed in its intended context, *The Recluse,* of which only fragments were completed.

The 1850 *Prelude*, published just ten weeks after his death, represents three major revisions and several minor ones. In this last version, Wordsworth refined the more ecstatic parts and suppressed the poem's radical statements about the supremacy of the human mind and its union with Nature. The 1805 and the 1850 versions are not radically different, however, so it is easy to speak about the latter two versions simultaneously. Many scholars believe that Wordsworth damaged the 1805 *Prelude* in his attempt to improve and polish it. Wordsworth's political views and poetic vision changed slowly, but radically, over the course of his lifetime. The young Wordsworth and the old Wordsworth are often discussed as two different artists—the younger being far more vital and significant. The young Wordsworth was a revolutionary, semi-atheist, and humanist. The old Wordsworth was a conservative, defender of Church and State, though certainly still a humanist. It is not debatable, however, that his genius manifested itself within a single decade in late youth: 1798 to 1808.

What he wrote before and after this decade would have given him a place in literary history, but certainly not the one he wanted and won, the one next to Milton. Throughout his life, Wordsworth was driven by the desire to match and surmount his literary predecessor, John Milton, and in particular Milton's epic, *Paradise Lost. The Prelude* is Wordsworth's answer to *Paradise Lost.*

In *The Prelude,* Wordsworth sets up a cycle of development, crisis, and recovery. This recovery moves him to a state of existence higher than the initial one—there is an added sense of awe, a heightened awareness. This new sensitivity gives meaning to human existence where there was none before, where there was only suffering and loss. The central philosophical question of *The Prelude* is answered—how to understand human existence in the quagmire of decline and destruction we see everywhere around us.

Throughout the poem are "spots of time," as Wordsworth called them. These were intense, revelatory, almost hallucinogenic moments that descended on him occasionally, in natural surroundings, bringing him closer to nature, helping him comprehend it and define his own relationship to it.

The poem is climaxed by two revelations. At Cambridge, he achieves an inward knowledge that he is a kind of chosen one, and on a walk home from a dance during a summer dawn he experiences a "spot of time":

> Ah, need I say, dear friend, that to the brim
> My heart was full? I made no vows, but vows
> Were then made for me: bond unknown to me
> Was given, that I should be—else sinning greatly—
> A dedicated spirit. On I walked
> In blessedness, which even yet remains. (Book 4, lines 333–339)

This was the first revelation. His futile commitment to the French Revolution comprises a part of his subsequent despair, but it also gives him the insight that he was not going to be a "spirit" of deeds.

> Above all
> Did Nature bring again this wiser mood,
> More deeply reestablished in my soul,
> Which, seeing little worthy or sublime
> In what we blazon with the pompous names
> Of power and action, early tutored me
> To look with feelings of fraternal love
> Upon those unassuming things that hold
> A silent station in this beauteous world. (Book 12, lines 38–47)

His role would necessitate a seclusion, a withdrawal, a solitary lifestyle that would allow him the detachment he needed to meditate. His role was to extend the meaning of poetry and bring nature to those who cannot see it:

> Prophets of Nature, we to them will speak
> A lasting inspiration, sanctified
> By reason and by truth; what we have loved
> Others will love, and we may teach them how: (Book 13, lines 446–449)

Wordsworth's despair sprang also from his search for identity, which was resolved in the discovery of his purpose. The twelfth book of *The Prelude* articulates his ideas for the revolution of poetry that he wanted to bring about, particularly with regards to subjects, style, and values. *The Prelude* incorporates the discovery of its own self, its own reason for being. It articulates the achievement of "Vision."

The second revelation is described in the concluding book of *The Prelude*. It is achieved on top of Mount Snowdown, an experience Wordsworth had in 1791, before his adventures in France, but is placed achronologically at the end of the poem. Wordsworth breaks through cloud cover and sees a scene of immense beauty. Then, later that night:

> A meditation rose in me that night
> Upon the lonely mountain when the scene
> Had passed away, and it appeared to me
> The perfect image of the mighty mind,
> Of one that feeds upon infinity,
> That is exalted by an under-presence (Book 13, lines 67–72)

Wordsworth decided to "create/ A like existence." What has been revealed to Wordsworth in this landscape is the focus of the planned poem, *The Recluse*—the mind of Man, the union between the mind and the external world.

The whole poem is achronological, beginning at the end, when he has chosen to take up residence at Grasmere. He does not tell the story as if it were set in the past, but in the present as he looks backward at the events of his life as well as the small moments of spontaneity, the sensations, the fleeting emotions and impressions that filled his childhood and his formative years. He speaks of a former self and the altered present self as two beings rather than the progression of one. In this Wordsworth achieves a mixed and manifold awareness that he calls two consciousnesses. The idea of memory weaves itself through much of Wordsworth's poetry, but memory takes on a new and more profound meaning as he discovers that its nature is more complicated than a mere record of past events:

Which yet have such self-practice in the mind
That sometimes when I think of them I seem
Two consciousnesses—conscious of myself
And of some other being.   (Book 2, lines 30–33)

His aim was to capture the freshness of first sensation before it was downtrodden by routine.

But Wordsworth's vision of an earthly paradise faded over the course of his lifetime. He could not maintain his closeness to nature and his awe of the mind of man. He became didactic in many of his later poems, his humanism turning into overt lessons or lectures given to those who did not have empathy for the common man. He worried often that his muse had left him in his later years:

Oh, yet a few short years of useful life,
And all will be complete–thy race run,
Thy monument of glory will be raised.
Then, though too weak to tread the ways of truth,
This age fall back to old idolatry.
Though men return to servitude as fast
As the tide ebbs, to ignominy and shame
By nations sink together, we shall still
Find solace in the knowledge which we have (Book 13, lines 432–440)

NOTE: All quotes from "The Prelude" are from the 1805 "Prelude" as it appears in *The Prelude, 1799, 1805, 1850,* eds. Jonathan Wordsworth, M. H. Abrams, and Stephen Gill. (New York: W.W. Norton and Company, 1979)

Critical Views on
"The Prelude"

A. C. BRADLEY ON THE ORIGINALITY OF WORDSWORTH

[A. C. Bradley, Professor of Poetry at Oxford, wrote *Shakespearean Tragedy* (1904) and *Oxford Lectures on Poetry* (1909).]

There have been greater poets than Wordsworth, but none more original. He saw new things, or he saw things in a new way. Naturally, this would have availed us little if his new things had been private fancies, or if his new perception had been superficial. But that was not so. If it had been, Wordsworth might have won acceptance more quickly, but he would not have gained his lasting hold on poetic minds. As it is, those in whom he creates the taste by which he is relished, those who learn to love him (and in each generation they are not a few), never let him go. Their love for him is of the kind that he himself celebrated, a settled passion, perhaps "slow to begin," but "never ending," and twined around the roots of their being. And the reason is that they find his way of seeing the world, his poetic experience, what Arnold meant by his "criticism of life," to be something deep, and therefore something that will hold. It continues to bring them joy, peace, strength, exaltation. It does not thin out or break beneath them as they grow older and wiser; nor does it fail them, much less repel them, in sadness or even in their sorest need. And yet—to return to our starting-point—it continues to strike them as original, and something more. It is not like Shakespeare's myriad-mindedness; it is, for good or evil or both, peculiar. They can remember, perhaps, the day when first they saw a cloud somewhat as Wordsworth saw it, or first really understood what made him write this poem or that; his unique way of seeing and feeling, though now familiar and beloved, still brings them not only peace, strength, exaltation, but a "shock of mild surprise"; and his paradoxes, long known by heart and found full of truth, still remain paradoxes.

If this is so, the road into Wordsworth's mind must be through his strangeness and his paradoxes, and not round them. I do not mean that they are everywhere in his poetry. Much of it, not to speak of occasional platitudes, is beautiful without being peculiar or difficult;

and some of this may be as valuable as that which is audacious or strange. But unless we get hold of that, we remain outside Wordsworth's centre; and, if we have not a most unusual affinity to him, we cannot get hold of that unless we realise its strangeness, and refuse to blunt the sharpness of its edge. Consider, for example, two or three of his statements; the statements of a poet, no doubt, and not of a philosopher, but still evidently statements expressing, intimating, or symbolizing, what for him was the most vital truth. He said that the meanest flower that blows could give him thoughts that often lie too deep for tears. He said, in a poem not less solemn, that Nature was the soul of all his moral being; and also that she can so influence us that nothing will be able to disturb our faith that all that we behold is full of blessings. After making his Wanderer tell the heart-rending tale of Margaret, he makes him say that the beauty and tranquillity of her ruined cottage had once so affected him

> That what we feel of sorrow and despair
> From ruin and from change, and all the grief
> The passing shows of Being leave behind,
> Appeared an idle dream, that could not live
> Where meditation was.
> [*The Excursion*, I, 949–53]

—A. C. Bradley, "Wordsworth," in *Oxford Lectures on Poetry*, 2nd ed. (London: Macmillan and Company, 1950): pp. 13–14.

LIONEL TRILLING ON THE SENTIMENT OF BEING

[Lionel Trilling is University Professor at Columbia. His critical writings include *Matthew Arnold* (1939), *The Liberal Imagination* (1950), *The Opposing Self* (1955), and *Beyond Culture: Essays on Learning and Literature* (1965).]

In *The Prelude*, in Book Two, Wordsworth speaks of a particular emotion which he calls "the sentiment of Being." The "sentiment" has been described in this way: "There is, in sanest hours, a consciousness, a thought that rises, independent, lifted out from all else, calm, like the stars, shining eternal. This is the thought of identity—yours for you, whoever you are, as mine for me. Miracle of miracles, beyond statement, most spiritual and vaguest of earth's dreams, yet hardest basic fact, and only entrance to all facts." This, of course, is not Wordsworth, it is Walt Whitman, but I quote Whitman's statement in exposition of Wordsworth's "sentiment of Being" because it is in some respects rather more boldly explicit, although not necessarily better, than anything that Wordsworth himself wrote about the sentiment, and because Whitman goes on to speak of his "hardest basic fact" as a political fact, as the basis, and the criterion, of democracy.

Through all his poetic life Wordsworth was preoccupied by the idea, by the sentiment, by the problem, of being. All experience, all emotions lead to it. He was haunted by the mysterious fact that he existed. He could discover in himself different intensities and qualities of being—"Tintern Abbey" is the attempt to distinguish these intensities and qualities. Being is sometimes animal; sometimes it is an "appetite and a passion"; sometimes it is almost a suspension of the movement of the breath and blood. The *Lyrical Ballads* have many intentions, but one of the chief of them is the investigation of the problems of being. "We are Seven," which is always under the imputation of bathos, is established in its true nature when we read it as an ontological poem; its subject is the question, What does it mean when we say a person is ? "The Idiot Boy," which I believe to be a great and not a foolish poem, is a kind of comic assertion of the actuality—and, indeed, the peculiar intensity—of being in a person who is outside the range of anything but our merely mechanical understanding. Johnny on the little horse, flourishing his branch of holly under the moon, is a creature of rapture, who, if he is not quite "human," is certainly elemental, magical, perhaps a little divine—"It was Johnny, Johnny everywhere." As much as anyone, and more than many—more than most—he *is*, and feels that he is.

From even the little I have said, it will be seen that as soon as the "sentiment of Being" is named, or represented, there arises a question of its degree of actuality or of its survival. "The glad animal movements" of the boy, the "appetite" and the "passion" of the young man's response to Nature easily confirm the sense of being. So do those experiences which are represented as a "sleep" or "slumber," when the bodily senses are in abeyance. But as the man grows older the stimuli to the experience of the sentiment of being grow fewer or grow less intense—it is this fact rather than any question of poetic creation (such as troubled Coleridge) that makes the matter of the "Immortality Ode." Wordsworth, as it were, puts the awareness of being to the test in situations where its presence may perhaps most easily be questioned—in very old people. Other kinds of people also serve for the test, such as idiots, the insane, children, the dead, but I emphasize the very old because Wordsworth gave particular attention to them, and because we can all be aware from our own experience what a strain very old people put upon our powers of attributing to them personal being, "identity." Wordsworth's usual way is to represent the old man as being below the human condition, apparently scarcely able to communicate, and then suddenly, startlingly, in what we have learned to call an "epiphany," to show forth the intensity of his human existence. The old man in "Animal Tranquillity and Decay" is described as being so old and so nearly inanimate that the birds regard him as little as if he were a stone or a tree; for this, indeed, he is admired, and the poem says that his unfelt peace is so perfect that it is envied by the very young. He is questioned about his destination on the road—

> I asked him whither he was bound, and what
> The object of his journey; he replied,
> "Sir! I am going many miles to take
> A last leave of my son, a mariner,
> Who from a sea-fight has been brought to Falmouth,
> And there is dying in a hospital."

The revelation of the actuality of his being, of his humanness, quite dazzles us.

—Lionel Trilling, "Wordsworth and the Iron Time," in *Wordsworth: Centenary Studies Presented at Cornell and Princeton Universities* (Princeton, N.J.: Princeton University Press, 1951): pp. 57–58.

GEOFFREY H. HARTMAN ON THE ROMANCE OF NATURE

[Geoffrey Hartman is Professor of English and Comparative Literature at Yale. His books include *The Unmediated Vision* (1954), *Wordsworth's Poetry, 1787–1814* (1964), and *Beyond Formalism: Literary Essays, 1958–1970* (1970).]

Nature, for Wordsworth, is not an "object" but a presence and a power; a motion and a spirit; not something to be worshiped and consumed, but always a guide leading beyond itself. This guidance starts in earliest childhood. The boy of *Prelude* I is fostered alike by beauty and by fear. Through beauty, nature often makes the boy feel at home, for, as in the Great Ode, his soul is alien to this world. But through fear, nature reminds the boy from where he came, and prepares him, having lost heaven, also to lose nature. The boy of *Prelude* I, who does not yet know he must suffer this loss as well, is warned by nature itself of the solitude to come.

I have suggested elsewhere how the fine skating scene of the first book, though painted for its own sake, to capture the animal spirits of children spurred by a clear and frosty night, moves from vivid images of immediate life to an absolute calm which foreshadows a deeper and more hidden life. The Negative Way is a gradual one, and the child is weaned by a premonitory game of hide-and-seek in which nature changes its shape from familiar to unfamiliar, or even fails the child. There is a great fear, either in Wordsworth or in nature, of traumatic breaks: *Natura non facit saltus.*

If the child is led by nature to a more deeply meditated understanding of nature, the mature singer who composes *The Prelude* begins with that understanding or even beyond it—with the spontaneously creative spirit. Wordsworth plunges into *media res*, where the *res* is Poetry, or Nature only insofar as it has guided him to a height whence he must find his own way. But Book VI, with which we are immediately concerned, records what is chronologically an intermediate period, in which the first term is neither Nature nor Poetry. It is Imagination in embryo: the mind muted yet also strengthened by the external world's opacities. Though imagination is with Wordsworth in the journey of 1790, nature seems particularly elusive. He goes out to a nature which seems to hide as in the crossing of the Alps.

The first part of this episode is told to illustrate a curious melancholy related to the "presence" of imagination and the "absence" of nature. Like the young Apollo in Keats's *Hyperion*, Wordsworth is strangely dissatisfied with the riches before him, and compelled to seek some other region:

> Where is power?
> Whose hand, whose essence, what divinity
> Makes this alarum in the elements,
> While I here idle listen on the shores
> In fearless yet in aching ignorance?

To this soft or "luxurious" sadness, a more masculine kind is added, which results from a "stern mood" or "underthirst of vigor"; and it is in order to throw light on this further melancholy that Wordsworth tells the incident of his crossing of the Alps.

—Geoffrey H. Hartman, "The Romance of Nature and the Negative Way," in *Wordsworth's Poetry 1787–1814* (New Haven, Conn.: Yale University Press, 1954): pp. 40–41.

JONATHAN WORDSWORTH ON THE TWO-PART *PRELUDE* OF 1799

[Jonathan Wordsworth, a descendant of the poet's brother Christopher, is the University Lecturer in Romantic Studies at Oxford, Fellow of St. Catherine's College, and Chairman of the Wordsworth Trust, Grasmere. He is the author of *The Music of Humanity: A Critical Study of Wordsworth's "Ruined Cottage"* (1969) and of *William Wordsworth: The Borders of Vision* (1982).]

The two-part *Prelude* in fact offers in a simpler and more concentrated form much of what one thinks of as best in the thirteen-Book poem. It does not constitute an alternative to 1805, but in so far as Wordsworth's vision of childhood is the inspiration and sustaining force of all versions of *The Prelude*, 1799 has outstanding claims. Lacking, of course, are the experiences of Wordsworth's young manhood, the moment of consecration in Book VI (with the famous lines upon imagination and the Simplon Pass), and the climactic Ascent of Snowdon from Book XIII, but almost all the childhood "spots of time" are to be found, and found in their original sequence. The presence of the additional "spots" give the poetry extraordinary power—the fact that in Part I after the woodcock-snaring, birds-nesting, boat-stealing, and skating episodes of Book I, there are the Drowned Man, the woman with her garments vexed and tossed, and the Waiting for the Horses, still to come. But even more important is the effect of returning Wordsworth's famous definition to its original place.

As it stands in Book XI of 1805, the assertion "There are in our existence spots of time . . .", though of course highly impressive, is removed a very long way from the poetry of Book I with which it had originally been connected, and has to take a structural weight that it cannot easily bear. In 1799, by contrast, it is at the centre of Wordsworth's thinking—a support alike for his faith in the value of primal experience, and for the further definition of Part II as he goes on to explore more fully the role of imagination. In its early form the passage is brief and to the point, half the length of the more pompous later version:

> There are in our existence spots of time
> Which with distinct preeminence retain
> A fructifying virtue, whence, depressed
> By trivial occupations and the round
> Of ordinary intercourse, our minds—
> Especially the imaginative power—
> Are nourished and invisibly repaired;
> Such moments chiefly seem to have their date
> In our first childhood.

—Jonathan Wordsworth, "The Growth of a Poet's Mind," in *The Cornell Library Journal* 11 (Spring 1970): pp. 7–8.

M. H. Abrams on *The Prelude* and *The Recluse*

[M. H. Abrams, the renowned scholar of romanticism, is Professor of English at Cornell. His writings on the romantic period include *The Mirror and the Lamp: Romantic Theory and the Critical Tradition* (1953) and *Natural Supernaturalism: Tradition and Revolution in Romantic Literature* (1971).]

Wordsworth does not tell his life as a simple narrative in past time but as the present remembrance of things past, in which forms and sensations "throw back our life" and evoke the former self which coexists with the altered present self in a multiple awareness that Wordsworth calls "two consciousnesses." There is a wide "vacancy" between the I now and the I then,

> Which yet have such self-presence in my mind
> That, sometimes, when I think of them, I seem
> Two consciousnesses, conscious of myself
> And of some other Being.

The poet is aware of the near impossibility of disengaging "the naked recollection of that time" from the intrusions of "after-meditation." In a fine and subtle figure for the interdiffusion of the two consciousnesses, he describes himself as one bending from a drifting boat on a still water, perplexed to distinguish actual objects at the bottom of the lake from surface reflections of the environing scene, from the tricks and refractions of the water currents, and from his own intrusive but inescapable image (that is, his present awareness). Thus "incumbent o'er the surface of past time" the poet, seeking the elements of continuity between his two disparate selves, conducts a persistent exploration of the nature and significance of memory, of his power to sustain freshness of sensation and his "first creative sensibility" against the deadening effect of habit and analysis, and of manifestations of the enduring and the eternal within the realm of change and time. Only intermittently does the narrative order coincide with the order of actual occurrence. Instead Wordsworth proceeds by sometimes bewildering ellipses, fusion, and as he says, "motions retrograde" in time.

Scholars have long been aware that it is perilous to rely on the factual validity of *The Prelude*, and in consequence Wordsworth has been charged with intellectual uncertainty, artistic ineptitude, bad memory, or even bad faith. The poem has suffered because we know so much about the process of its composition between 1798 and 1805—its evolution from a constituent part to a "tail-piece" to a "portico" of *The Recluse*, and Wordsworth's late decision to add to the beginning and end of the poem the excluded middle: his experiences in London and France. A work is to be judged, however, as a finished and free-standing product; and in *The Prelude* as it emerged after six years of working and reworking, the major alterations and dislocations of the events of Wordsworth's life are imposed deliberately, in order that the design inherent in that life, which has become apparent only to his mature awareness, may stand revealed as a principle which was invisibly operative from the beginning. A supervising idea, in other words, controls Wordsworth's account and shapes it into a structure in which the protagonist is put forward as one who has been elected to play a special role in a providential plot. As

Wordsworth said in the opening passage, which represents him after he has reached maturity: in response to the quickening outer breeze

> to the open fields I told
> A prophecy: poetic numbers came
> Spontaneously, and cloth'd in priestly robe
> My spirit, thus singled out, as it might seem,
> For holy services.

Hence in this history of a poet's mind the poet is indeed the "transitory Being," William Wordsworth, but he is also the exemplary poet-prophet who has been singled out, in a time "of hopes o'erthrown . . . of dereliction and dismay," to bring mankind tidings of comfort and joy; as Wordsworth put it in one version of the Prospectus,

> that my verse may live and be
> Even as a light hung up in heaven to chear
> Mankind in times to come.

—M. H. Abrams, *Natural Supernaturalism: Tradition and Revolution in Romantic Literature* (New York: W. W. Norton and Company, 1971): pp. 158–159.

RICHARD ONORATO ON NATURE AND "THE PRELUDE"

[Richard Onorato is the author of *The Character of a Poet: Wordsworth in* The Prelude.]

He remembers, too, that the pure pleasure of childish play seemed to absorb the beauty of the surroundings; and he says explicitly that in this way Nature "*Peopled* my mind with beauteous forms or grand / And made me love them . . . ," just as the ambience of the mother's love had once suffused the natural objects of the world for the infant with light, love, and wonder. (Notice, too, that "peopled" figuratively preserves in the beauteous forms of Nature a very human association.) And Wordsworth himself surmises that Nature's way of doing this for the child is a further development of the mother-infant relationship:

> those first-born affinities that fit
> our new existence to existing things,
> And, in our dawn of being, constitute
> The bond of union betwixt life and joy.

The "ghostly language of the ancient earth" heard in solitude in the windy darkness is a projection into Nature of a preconscious sense of a lost relationship, of the dialogue that the infant had with the mother's heart. Nature metaphorically "speaking" to him in solitude, wind, and darkness makes him want to speak that "visionary" language which he tells us later is poetry. To speak of visionary things is to use the imagination to evoke, and perhaps subsequently recognize, lost objects of love and wonder, to reveal in special utterance their ghostly or shadowy existence in the mind, called elsewhere "those phantoms of conceit," "the many feelings that oppressed my heart."

Here, too, we should notice how "heart" is associated with the mother and death. "Mute dialogues with my mother's *heart*" calls to mind: "the heart / And hinge of all our learning and our loves . . ." and "our being's heart and home is with infinitude. . . ." A revision made by Wordsworth in the Poetry passage from Book V suggests further that it is a knowledge of what has been lost in death that poetry might uncover and present ("as objects recognized in flashes") when the poet's ability to speak in a visionary way matches his sense of being spoken to. When he changes "the motions of the winds" to "the motions of the *viewless* winds," I think that he is also preconsciously recalling Claudio's speech from *Measure for Measure*, which supplies the context of the imagination attempting to deal with the fear of death as an incomprehensible journey:

> Ay, but to die, and go we know not where;
> To lie in cold obstruction and to rot;
> This sensible war motion to become
> A kneaded clod, and the delighted spirit
> To bathe in fiery floods, or to reside
> In thrilling region of thick-ribbed ice;
> To be imprison'd in the viewless winds,
> And blown with restless violence round about
> The pendent world . . .

Death and darkness are associated with the "*ghostly* language of the ancient earth" and with the "viewless winds" of poetry. But illuminating light and glory are also associated with poetry. We remember from Book II that the "one belov'd Presence," which so closely resembles the "Presence" in Nature of "Tintern Abbey," is one that "*irradiates* and exalts . . . all objects through all intercourse of sense"; and this, I think, suggests why poetry is also said to have a "light divine" which suffuses objects and presents them "in flashes," whereas there is a darkness inherent in language.

—Richard J. Onorato, *The Character of the Poet: William Wordsworth in "The Prelude"* (Princeton, N.J.: Princeton University Press, 1971): pp. 114–115.

THOMAS WEISKEL ON WORDSWORTH AND IMAGINATION

[The late Thomas Weiskel taught English at Yale. His *The Romantic Sublime* was published posthumously.]

Wordsworth was not a symbolic poet and not a descriptive poet either, if indeed a poet can be descriptive. His landscapes hover on the edge of revelation without revealing anything, and so the very moment of hovering, of glimpsed entry into the beyond, when "the light of sense / Goes out, but with a flash that has revealed / The invisible world," usurps the missing climax of symbolic revelation. In the Snowdon version, for example, the salient elements of that magnificent scene—the suspended moon, the sea of hoary mist, the blue chasm in the vapor—refuse to harden into symbolic equation with the imagination or anything else, as Geoffrey Hartman has observed. And this is so despite the fact the Wordsworth is there working explicitly with notions of analogy, type, and emblem. So too with that spot of time when the young boy, having lost his way while riding near Penrith, sees a naked pool, the beacon on the summit, and the girl with a pitcher forcing her way against the wind—salient images which are less than symbols and all the more powerful for that. Or the schoolboy in his mountain lookout, waiting to be fetched home for a holiday that turned into a funeral, who later finds himself returning to certain "kindred spectacles and sounds"—

> . . . the wind and sleety rain,
> And all the business of the elements,
> The single sheep, and the one blasted tree,
> And the bleak music from that old stone wall,
> The noise of wood and water, and the mist
> That on the line of each of those two roads
> Advanced in such indisputable shapes

—thence to drink as at a fountain. Many instances of such salience could be adduced, but this feature of Wordsworth's landscapes is widely appreciated and is here evoked only to suggest the scope of the moment we wish to isolate. If the images so projected into the field of Wordsworth's past were to lose their opacity and become the transparent signifiers of an invisible world, the soul would "remember" what she felt and have nothing to pursue. The conversation, propelled as it is by the baffled misconstruction of the signifier, would be over; Wordsworth would understand himself. Indeed, as the poem goes on Wordsworth is less and less disposed to interrogate the images that rise upon him. The gestures of self-inquisition become the mere feinting of a mind learning how knowledge is opposed to efficacious power.

Visionary power is associated with the transcendence of the image and in particular with the "power in sound"; yet it depends upon a resistance within that transcendence of sight for sound. In the Wordsworthian moment two events appear to coalesce: the withdrawal or the occultation of the image and the epiphany of the character or signifier proper. A form or image may be installed in either the imaginative or symbolic domains. There is a world of difference between the two, but the differentiation can never be found within the image itself. If an image is symbolic, that fact is signaled by what we loosely call "context"—its inscription in an order or language whose structure is prior to its meaning (signifieds) and so determines it. On the other hand, an image (fantasy or perception) may fall short of the symbolic, in which case it remains opaque and meaningless in itself. Earlier we spoke of rememoration as a confrontation with a signifier, but strictly speaking, an image becomes a signifier only when it is recognized as such, and this may involve imputing an intentionality to the image. (A homely example: a child responds to pictures or the type in a book only as colors and shapes until the magical moment when he discerns that they are representations; it is the displaced recapitulation of this moment that is in question here.) There is implicit in the passage from imagination to symbol a confrontation with symbolicity—the very fact of structure in its priority and independent of its actual organization. Hence the signifier may be misconstrued in two possible ways. It may be simply misread, or—and this is in point with Wordsworth—there may be a resistance or a barrier to its recognition as a signifier, a resistance to reading itself as opposed to seeing. I think the resistance may be identified with what Wordsworth calls imagination.

—Thomas Weiskel, "Wordsworth and the Defile of the Word," in *The Romantic Sublime: Studies in the Structure and Psychology of Trancendence* (Baltimore: Johns Hopkins University Press, 1976): pp. 100–101.

KENNETH R. JOHNSTON ON "HOME AT GRASMERE" IN 1800

[Kenneth R. Johnston is Professor of English at Indiana University, and the author of *Wordsworth and* The Recluse.]

The identification of William Wordsworth with the English Lake District is so elemental a fact of literary history that one easily forgets there was a time when the fact had to be created in competition with other available options. Despite the fine biographical and poetical inevitability of the Wordsworths' move to Grasmere, the principals in the case were by no means sure of destiny's direction. In their correspondence of 1798–99, the question of where to settle (closely linked to questions of what to do) is indeed preeminent; but by far the most important variable was how to remain close to Coleridge. Grasmere and the Lakes entered into the decision belatedly, as an entertaining diversion. Once their dissatisfaction with Germany had set in (December 1798), Dorothy wrote to Coleridge that they should all explore together "every nook of that romantic country" the following summer, "wherever we finally settle." Coleridge, during the whole year, held out for the south as being better for Wordsworth because it was nearer the intellectual company he felt Wordsworth needed more than books. In July he reported with disappointment that Wordsworth "renounces Alfoxden altogether," but William and Dorothy's letters indicate no clear alternative except for "William's wish to be near a good library, and if possible in a pleasant country."

These domestic decisions are important poetically as well as biographically because they help to explain the peculiarly aggressive vehemence of Wordsworth's joy in the portions of "Home at Grasmere" written in the spring of 1800 as a fresh start on *The Recluse*. There is undoubtedly creative psychological significance in the curious fact that almost all major segments of *The Recluse* were undertaken when the Wordsworths had just completed, or were just beginning to contemplate, a move to a new home—and, moreover, that this occurred with each of the residences they occupied from Alfoxden on. That this is more than mere coincidence is strongly suggested by one of the poet's few post-1815 efforts to work on his masterpiece, "Composed When a Probability Existed of Our Being Obliged to Quit Rydal Mount as a Residence," 1826, a meditation of over two hundred lines in which *The Recluse*'s frequent discrepancy between grand themes and small occasions is especially marked. In 1800, the Wordsworths were not returning home to Grasmere but going to Grasmere as if it were home, a situation "conducive to a self-conscious awareness of himself as an observer," not to the recapture of an "indigenous" childhood. Their seven-month stay with the Hutchinson family at Sockburn had shown them brothers and sisters reunited as a happy, independent family of adults, a potent image because of their own painful childhood memories of being scattered abroad after the death of their father in 1783. They had also been living for four years in what seemed to their elder relations a state of semivagabondage and were very eager to stop it. The question of Wordsworth's career—indeed, of his profession—was crucial in deciding where to go from the temporary hospitality of the Hutchinson farm. Careers were not to be made in Grasmere; not the least of Wordsworth's imaginative achievements was his establishment of a national literary reputation from so remote a provincial spot. Cowper and Collins and others may have suggested models, but they were gentlemanly recluses on church, university, or family sinecures, and in any case they did not plan to save the world with their poetry. The November walking tour was not the summer vacation jaunt Dorothy had proposed but an effort to interest Coleridge on the North; yet it also had the effect of allowing Wordsworth to see the Lakes with newly approving eyes—Coleridge's. His letter back to Dorothy at Sockburn concentrates on Coleridge's responses—"Coleridge enchanted with Grasmere and Rydal"—and Coleridge's enthusiasm catalyzes his own: "Coleridge was much struck with Grasmere and its neighbourhood and I have much to say to you, you will think my plan a mad one, but I have thought of building a house by the Lake side . . ." Barely a month before the great move "home" to Grasmere, the idea struck its proposer "mad," as it surely must have seemed to his relatives and to received ideas of how and where a not-so-young man of uncertain promise would establish his independence in the world. Nor was the author of "The Mad Mother," "Incipient Madness," and other lyrics of the psychopathology of everyday life likely to use the word with sophisticated frivolity.

William and Dorothy's return in December of 1799 was full of wonder and loving observation. They were returning, brother and sister, aged twenty-nine and twenty-seven, to the general neighborhood of their childhood, reentering after long absence a childhood dream. The reestablishment of their feelings for this landscape was inextricably tied up with the re-formation of their family.

—Kenneth R. Johnston, "'Home at Grasmere' in 1800" in *Wordsworth and* The Recluse (New Haven, Conn.: Yale University Press, 1984): pp. 173–175.

Thematic Analysis of
"Tintern Abbey" and the *Lyrical Ballads*

The Advertisement to the *Lyrical Ballads* of 1798 describes the poems as experiments that were written to ascertain "how far language of conversation in the middle and lower classes of society is adapted to the purposes of poetic pleasure." Wordsworth intended to give voice to those who, in English poetry, had not had one before: the poor, the old, the infirm. However condescending his statement may sound to our ears today, the *Lyrical Ballads* are radical and humanist when viewed from the perspective of the time when they were written. These poems were innovative for their conversational style and their content emphasizing the imagination and nature, concentrating on "simple" subjects.

Published anonymously in 1798, the *Lyrical Ballads* were composed by both Wordsworth and his close friend, the poet Samuel Taylor Coleridge. Together, Coleridge and Wordsworth planned a volume of a new kind of poetry that Wordsworth carefully outlined in the Preface to the second edition of the *Lyrical Ballads*. They planned to write poetry of simplicity, naturalness, and spontaneity. Wordsworth warned his audience, "Readers accustomed to the gaudiness and inane phraseology of many modern writers, if they persist in reading this book to its conclusion, will perhaps frequently have to struggle with feelings of strangeness and awkwardness."

The volume begins with Coleridge's "Rime of the Ancient Mariner" and concludes with Wordsworth's "Tintern Abbey," (the true title being "Lines Composed a few Miles above Tintern Abbey"). There are twenty-three poems in the book, nineteen by Wordsworth and four by Coleridge.

Coleridge's "Rime of the Ancient Mariner" is now considered one of the finest poems in the English language, but Wordsworth eventually turned against it. He had helped plan it and left the writing of it to Coleridge, but he did not like the archaic language. Wordsworth's hope for the *Lyrical Ballads* was that they would emancipate poetry not only from the traditional subjects, but from overbearing pedantic language. "It is the honorable characteristic of Poetry," he said in the Advertisement, "that its materials are to be found in every subject that can interest the human mind."

Although the Preface to the *Lyrical Ballads* was written by Wordsworth, it is relevant to both him and Coleridge, and has become as important as the poems themselves. In this artistic manifesto, Wordsworth aggressively seeks to enlighten his readers, to force them to see the supremacy of man in nature, and to make way for his own experimentation. He argues the importance of the mind of man and its direct link to nature—the need for a freer, more direct mode of expression.

Wordsworth regards poetry as "the most philosophic of all writing: its object is truth, not individual and local, but general and operative." Unlike the biographer and the historian, the poet "writes under one restriction only, namely, the necessity of giving immediate pleasure to a human Being possessed of that information which may be expected of him, not as a lawyer, a physician, a mariner, an astronomer, or a natural philosopher, but as a Man."

In the Advertisement, he tells his readers that "they will look round for poetry, and will be induced to inquire by what species of courtesy these attempts can be permitted to assume that title." This bold assumption of the efficacy of his own poetry, however sublimated, does exhibit a need to explain his experiment. There is hesitation fronted by enormous pomposity. Wordsworth is also careful to confirm his belief in the traditional notions of imitation and imagination.

"Readers of superior judgement may disapprove of the style in which many of the pieces are executed. It will perhaps appear to them that the author has sometimes descended too low and that many of his expressions are too familiar, and not of sufficient dignity," Wordsworth writes in the Advertisement. He implores his audience to second guess themselves rather than his poetry, to throw away artifice and conventional codes. He is warning them that they must throw away assumptions if they want to read this poetry:

> The principal object then which I proposed to myself in these
> Poems was to make the incidents of common life interesting by tracing
> in them, truly though not ostentatiously, the primary laws of nature:
> chiefly as far as regards the manner in which we associate ideas in a state
> of excitement. Low and rustic life was generally chosen because in that
> situation the essential passions of the heart find a better soil in which
> they can attain their maturity, are less under restraint, and speak a plainer
> and more emphatic language; because in that situation our elementary
> feelings exist in a state of greater simplicity and consequently may be
> more accurately contemplated and more forcibly communicated

More than a justification of his own poetry and poetic methods, the Preface is Wordsworth's own theory of poetry. Wordsworth states that this is poetry of humanistic values, out of the European Enlightenment. He reduces the question, in the Preface, to its most minimal: "I ask what is meant by the word Poet?" The answer is as artless and profound as his poetry: "He is a man speaking to men." He does not hesitate to add, however, "He is a man, it is true, endued with more lively sensibility, more enthusiasm and tenderness, who has a greater knowledge of human nature and a more comprehensive soul, than are supposed to be common among mankind." Modesty is not a Wordsworthian attribute.

"Tintern Abbey"

"Tintern Abbey" was composed after a four-day ramble from Tintern to Bristol. As the *Lyrical Ballads* were being prepared by the printer for publication, "Tintern Abbey" was written and rushed to the printer for inclusion. The poem was written at a time in Wordsworth's life when he had rejected Godwin's philosophical teachings, which denied the power of the sense and the emotions in favor of reason. Wordsworth had been, in his youth, a devout follower of Godwin, who was also a humanist. While Wordsworth did remain close to some of Godwin's ideas, he broke with the idea of the supremacy of scientific reason, writing intentionally about those without classical knowledge and, in many cases, without any reason at all, such as "The Idiot Boy."

"Tintern Abbey" is a remembrance and in it Wordsworth has a revelation. Wordsworth comes upon a scene in nature that he has not encountered for five years:

> Though absent long,
> These forms of beauty have not been to me,
> As is a landscape to a blind man's eye:
> But oft, in lonely rooms, and mid the din
> Of towns and cities, I have owed to them,
> In hours of weariness, sensations sweet

Wordsworth experiences one of his "blessed moods" in which the sense of sight gives way to the greater sense of sound. For Wordsworth, nature is not an object to be seen, but a ubiquitous presence to be felt, a sound to be heard emanating from somewhere beyond itself. And it provides a kind of salvation.

> Until, the breath of this corporeal frame,
> And even the motion of our human blood
> Almost suspended, we are laid asleep
> In body, and become a living soul:
> While with an eye made quiet by the power
> Of harmony, and the deep power of joy,
> We see into the life of things.

He understands himself as a poet, and he understands the idea of reciprocity between the natural world and his own mind—this is a story that Wordsworth will tell again and again throughout his poetry. He will tell it again in *The Prelude*.

Wordsworth addresses his beloved sister, Dorothy, directly as apprehends the memory of this scene:

> Therefore let the moon
> Shine on thee in thy solitary walk;
> And let the misty mountain winds be free
> To blow against thee: and in after years,
> When these wild ecstasies shall be matured
> Into a sober pleasure, when thy mind
> Shall be a mansion for all lovely forms,
> Thy memory be as a dwelling-place
> For all sweet sounds and harmonies;

This poem celebrates nature and its restorative powers, and yet there is still loss and decay present as an undercurrent, particularly because it is a memory. A memory can never contain what the initial experience did. And even in nature he hears ruin in "the still, sad music of humanity." But Wordsworth still prefers memory and its extraordinary senses to the strict intellect. This is to say that Wordsworth prefers poetry, as he does not separate memory from poetry. As he says in the Preface, "Poetry is the breath and finer spirit of all knowledge; it is the impassioned expression which is in the countenance of all Science. Emphatically may it be said of the Poet, as Shakespeare hath said of man, 'that he looks before and after.'" ❀

Note: All quotations from Wordsworth's *Lyrical Ballads* are from the edition *Lyrical Ballads and Other Poems*, Ed. W. J. B Owen (New York: Oxford University Press, 1969).

Critical Views on
"Tintern Abbey" and the *Lyrical Ballads*

WILLIAM HAZLITT ON THE SPIRIT OF THE AGE

[William Hazlitt (1778–1839) was an English essayist and a contemporary of William Wordsworth. He is remembered particularly for his criticism of Shakespeare and dramatic literature of the Elizabethan age.]

No one has shown the same imagination in raiding trifles into importance: no one has displayed the same pathos in treating of the simplest feelings of the heart. Reserved, yet haughty, having no unruly or violent passions, (or those passions having been early suppressed,) Mr. Wordsworth has passed his life in solitary musing, or in daily converse with the face of nature. He exemplifies in an eminent degree the power of association; for his poetry has no other source or character. He has dwelt among pastoral scenes, till each object has become connected with a thousand feelings, a link in the chain of thought, a fibre of his own heart. Every one is by habit, and familiarity strongly attached to the place of his birth, or to objects that recall the most pleasing and eventful circumstances of his life. But to the author of the *Lyrical Ballads*, nature is a kind of home; and he may be said to take a personal interest in the universe. There is no image so insignificant that it has not in some mood or other found the way into his heart: no sound that does not awaken the memory of other years.

> To him the meanest flower that blows can give
> Thoughts that do often lie too deep for tears.

The daisy looks up to him with sparkling eye as an old acquaintance: the cuckoo haunts him with sounds of early youth not to be expressed: a linnet's nest startles him with boyish delight: an old withered thorn is weighed down with a heap of recollections: a grey cloak, seen on some wild moor, torn by the wind, or drenched in the rain, afterwards becomes an object of imagination to him: even the lichens on the rock have a life and being in his thoughts. He has described all these objects in a way and with an intensity of feeling that no one else had done before him, and has given a new view or aspect of nature. He is in this sense the most original poet now living, and the one whose writings could the least be spared: for they have no substitute elsewhere. The vulgar do not read them, the learned, who see all things through books, do not understand them, the great despise, the fashionable may ridicule them: but the author has created himself an interest in the heart of the retired and lonely student of nature, which can never die. Persons of this class will still continue to feel what he has felt: he has expressed what they might in vain wish to express, except with glistening eye and faultering [sic] tongue! There is a lofty philosophic tone, a thoughtful humanity, infused into his pastoral vein. Remote from the passions and events of the great world, he has communicated interest and dignity to the primal movements of the heart of man, and ingrafted his own conscious reflections on the casual thoughts of hinds and shepherds. Nursed amidst the grandeur of mountain scenery, he has stooped to have a nearer view of the daisy under his feet, or plucked a branch of white-thorn from the spray: but in describing it, his mind seems imbued with the majesty of and solemnity of the objects around him—the tall rock lifts its head in the erectness of his spirit; the cataract roars in the sound of his verse; and in its dim and mysterious meaning, the mists seem to gather in the hollows of Helvellyn, and the forked Skiddaw hovers in the distance. There is little mention of mountainous scenery in Mr. Wordsworth's poetry; but by internal evidence one might be almost sure that it was written in a mountainous country, from its bareness, its simplicity, its loftiness and its depth . . .

—William Hazlitt, *The Spirit of the Age* and *English Poets*, 1825.

HELEN DARBISHIRE ON THE *LYRICAL BALLARDS* AND POEMS OF 1807

[Helen Darbishire, a noted Wordsworth scholar, wrote *The Poet Wordsworth* in 1950.]

'It is the honorable characteristic of poetry', he said, in the Advertisement to the *Lyrical Ballads*, 'that its materials are to be found in every subject that can interest the human mind.' He emancipated the poetic subject; and he brought back poetic language to its source in the living tongue. Thanks to Wordsworth, Browning could take as subject Mr. Sludge the medium no less than Fra Lippo Lippi. Tennyson could develop a rustic theme with even a banal simplicity:

'Take your own time, Annie, take your own time.'

And our twentieth-century poets can sweep, as we know, from Byzantine glories to damp housemaids on area steps, and can freely explore the possibilities of a poetic language which may range from the charged words of inscrutable nursery rhymes through every compelling idiosyncrasy of elliptical speech to the allusive lingo of learned scholarship.

But to read Wordsworth aright we must enter his poetic world as if we entered it for the first time, and I would urge that we should enter first into the world he reveals in that volume of 1798. It breathes the freshness of mountain air, the poetry seems to come from the earth like a mountain spring: its language is as colourless as water. The poet is looking into the heart of man and into the life of nature as if indeed he saw things for the first time:

> You look round on your mother earth . . .
> As if you were her first-born birth,
> And none had lived before you.

If he cannot give you this sense of the miracle of life, he gives you nothing.

A beginner might be advised to start at the end of the volume and read first the poem that was written last, *Lines written a few miles above Tintern Abbey*, where Wordsworth reveals what lies behind the sturdy faith in truth and fact of the *Lyrical Ballads*. Now in any of these ballad poems we may catch at moments a glimpse of something behind and beyond the story and its scene: it will generally come at the point where man and nature meet, the point in Wordsworth's inner experience where poetry is born. In 'one of the rudest of the ballads,' as Wordsworth called *Goody Blake and Harry Gill*, it comes when Goody kneels beneath the moon, and curses Harry Gill:

> The cold, cold moon above her head,
>   Thus on her knees did Goody pray.
> Young Harry heard what she had said,
>   And icy cold he turned away.

'The cold, cold moon above her head': there is a strange vibration here, as if the veil of reality were lifting, as if we not only saw an old woman caught stealing, but felt the whole universe in sympathy with her, as if for a moment we were living in another dimension, the dimension of the infinite.

Wordsworth said himself, 'In poetry it is the imaginative only, viz. that which is conversant with, or turns upon, infinity, that power-fully affects me.'

—Helen Darbishire, *The Poet Wordsworth* (Oxford: Clarendon Press, 1950): pp. 57-58.

ROBERT MAYO ON THE FAMILIARITY OF THE *LYRICAL BALLADS*

[Robert Mayo, Professor of English at Northwestern University, is the author of *The English Novel in the Magazines, 1740–1815* (1962).]

It is well to observe, in terminating this study, that those commentators who have emphasized the "originality" of the *Lyrical Ballads* to the exclusion of their many signs of contemporaneity, or who see the volume as a daring "manifesto" in total defiance of the general taste, overlook Coleridge's explicit statements to the contrary in the *Biographia Literaria*. Writing in 1815–16, at a time removed yet close enough to the event itself, he denied categorically that the *Lyrical Ballads* were "the original occasion of this fiction of a new school of poetry," or even that he and Southey had been the initiators of a tendency which extended back at least to Bowles and Cooper, among modern poets "the first who reconciled the heart with the head." In fact, he appears to support the literary orthodoxy of the *Ballads* in both subject and manner by insisting upon their overwhelming acceptability to the reading public of their time, saying that in his studied opinion at least two-thirds of the poems would have pleased the average reader, and that "the omission of less than a hundred lines [from the 437 pages of the 1800 edition] would have precluded nine-tenths of the criticism on this work"—supposing, of course, "that the reader has taken it up, *as he would have done any other collection of poems* [italics ours] purporting to derive their subjects or interests from the incidents of domestic or ordinary life, intermingled with higher strains of meditation which the poet utters in his own person and character." It was not the subjects or the manner which offended in the volume, according to Coleridge, but "the critical remarks" which were "prefixed and annexed" to it—remarks which were in part erroneous, which were greatly misunderstood, and which invited by their "supposed heresy" attacks from readers who otherwise would have accepted without question the greater part of the work itself.

Viewed casually, in other words, the *Lyrical Ballads* would tend to merge with familiar features of the literary landscape; read carefully, they would give suddenly a tremendous impression of clarity, freshness, and depth. Wordsworth's true genius was "the original gift of spreading the tone, atmosphere, and with it the depth and height of the ideal world around forms, incidents, and situations, of which, for the common view, custom had bedimmed all the lustre, had dried up the sparkle and the dewdrops." Coleridge is probably speaking here of the "forms, incidents, and situations" of real life, rather than of literature; but not necessarily so. It could be both. Certainly the poetry of the magazines was lusterless and stale. The "modifying colors" of Wordsworth's "imagination" could play over the "forms, incidents, and situations" reflected in contemporary verse, as well as those in the life behind it, and the record shows that they unquestionably did. Wordsworth's forte was not producing novelties, but operating in a new dimension where "original" combinations of "fixties and definites" were largely irrelevant. To claim more for his poetry, as some have done, would be for Coleridge to claim less. It would be to throw emphasis upon the *subjects* of his poetry, rather than its substance. It would be to confuse the "drapery" of poetic genius with its "soul." It would be to confound the superior powers of imagination with the inferior powers of fancy.

—Robert Mayo, "The Contemporaneity of the *Lyrical Ballads*," in *PMLA* 69 (1954): pp. 73–74.

[Stephen Maxfield Parrish, Professor of English at Cornell, is
coauthor (with Hyder Rollins) of *Keats and the Bostonians*
(1951) and author of *The Art of the Lyrical Ballads* (1972). He
is also general editor of the Cornell Wordsworth Series of editions, from the manuscripts, of all Wordsworth's long poems.]

That Wordsworth's design should have been lost sight of seems
astonishing, for he took unusual pains to make it clear. In the
"Advertisement" to the first edition of *Lyrical Ballads* he singled out
five poems for comment. Besides touching on the sources of three
and on the style of another, he had remarked meaningfully: "The
poem of the Thorn, as the reader will soon discover, is not supposed
to be spoken in the author's own person: the character of the loqua-
cious narrator will sufficiently shew itself in the course of the story."
In 1800, after the narrator's character had totally failed to show itself,
Wordsworth attached a lengthy note telling precisely what he had
intended to do in "The Thorn." He began by confessing that "this
Poem ought to have been preceded by an introductory Poem,"
implying that he would have sketched there the history of "The
Thorn's" narrator, then went on to supply the information that
poem might have contained. He asked the reader to visualize "a man,
a Captain of a small trading vessel, for example, who being past the
middle age of life, had retired . . . to some village or country town of
which he was not a native." Why a man of this sort? Because, the
poet explained, reaching his point deliberately and then summing it
up: "Such men, having little to do, become credulous and talkative
from indolence; and from the same cause, and other predisposing
causes . . . they are prone to superstition. On which account it
appeared to me proper to select a character like this to exhibit some
of the general laws by which superstition acts upon the mind."

Could any statement of poetic intent be plainer? As Wordsworth
conceived it, "The Thorn" is a portrayal of the superstitious imagination. More literally than any other poem, it carries out the principal
object of *Lyrical Ballads*: to trace in situations of common life "the
primary laws of our nature," chiefly "as regards the manner in which
we associate ideas in a state of excitement." For the manner in which
the narrator associates ideas is precisely what "The Thorn" is about.

The ideas themselves—that is, the "events" of the poem—are unimportant except as they reflect the working of the narrator's imagination. In fact, the point of the poem may very well be that its central "event" has no existence outside of the narrator's imagination—that there is no Martha Ray sitting in a scarlet cloak behind a crag on the mountain top, that the narrator has neither seen her nor heard her, that what he has seen is a gnarled old tree in a blinding storm, that what he has heard (besides the creaking of the branches, or the whistling of the mountain wind) is village superstition about a woman wronged years ago.

—Stephen Maxfield Parrish, "'The Thorn': Wordsworth's Dramatic Monologue," in *ELH* 24 (1957): pp. 154–155.

HAROLD BLOOM ON THE MYTH OF MEMORY AND NATURAL MAN

[Harold Bloom is Sterling Professor of the Humanities at Yale University and Professor of English at the New York University Graduate School. His books include *The Anxiety of Influence* (1973), *A Map of Misreading* (1975), and *The Western Canon* (1994).]

"Tintern Abbey" (July 1798) is a miniature of the long poem Wordsworth never quite wrote, the philosophical and autobiographical epic of which *The Prelude*, the *Recluse* fragment, and *The Excursion* would have been only parts. As such, "Tintern Abbey" is a history in little of Wordsworth's imagination. The procedure and kind of the poem are both determined by Coleridge's influence, for *The Eolian Harp* (1795) and *Frost at Midnight* (February 1798) are its immediate ancestors, with the eighteenth-century sublime ode in the farther background. Yet we speak justly of the form of "Tintern Abbey" as being Wordsworth's, for he turns this kind of poem to its destined theme, the nature of a poet's imagination and that imagination's relation to external Nature. Coleridge begins the theme in his "conversation poems," but allows himself to be distracted from it by theological misgivings and self-abnegation. "Tintern Abbey," and not

The Eolian Harp, is the father of Shelley's *Mont Blanc* and Keats's *Sleep and Poetry*.

In the renewed presence of a remembered scene, Wordsworth comes to a full understanding of his poetic self. This revelation, though it touches on infinity, is extraordinarily simple. All that Wordsworth learns by it is a principle of reciprocity between the external world and his own mind, but the story of that reciprocity becomes the central story of Wordsworth's best poetry. The poet loves Nature for its own sake alone, and the presences of Nature give beauty to the poet's mind, again only for that mind's sake. Even the initiative is mutual; neither Nature nor poet gives in hope of recompense, but out of this mutual generosity an identity is established between one giver's love and the other's beauty. The process of reciprocity is like a conversation that never stops, and cannot therefore be summed up discursively or analyzed into static elements. The most immediate consequence of this process is a certain "wide quietness," as Keats was to call it in his *Ode to Psyche*. As the dialogue of love and beauty ensues, love does not try to find an object, nor beauty an expression in direct emotion, but a likeness between man and Nature is suggested. The suggestion is made through an intensification of the dominant aspect of the given landscape, its seclusion, which implies also a deepening of the mood of seclusion in the poet's mind:

> —Once again
> Do I behold these steep and lofty cliffs,
> That on a wild secluded scene impress
> Thoughts of more deep seclusion; and connect
> The landscape with the quiet of the sky.

The further connection is with the quiet of Wordsworth's mind, for the thoughts of more deep seclusion are impressed simultaneously on the landscape and its human perceiver.

We murder to dissect, Wordsworth wrote in another context, and to dissect the renewed relationship between the poet and this particular landscape ought not to be our concern. Wordsworth wants to understand the interplay between Mind and Nature without asking how such dialogue can be, and this deliberate refusal to seek explanation is itself part of the meaning of "Tintern Abbey." The poet has reached a point where the thing seen yields to a clarity and we observe.

And observing is completing and we are content,
In a world that shrinks to an immediate whole,

That we do not need to understand, complete
Without secret arrangements of it in the mind.

—Harold Bloom, *The Visionary Company: A Reading of English Romantic Poetry* (Ithaca, N.Y.: Cornell University Press, 1971): pp. 95–96.

JOHN HOLLANDER ON WORDSWORTH AND THE MUSIC OF SOUND

[John Hollander is a poet and critic. He is Professor of English at Yale, where he also serves as Director of Graduate Studies in English. His criticism includes *Vision and Resonance* and *The Figure of Echo*. Much of his poetry is gathered in *Spectral Emanations: New and Selected Poems.*]

We need hardly be reminded, however, that the auditory realm is ever secondary to the kingdom of sight; and in these observations on the treatment of sound in Wordsworth's poetry, we shall be continually referred back to that secondariness by our want of a complementary term, in the aural dimension, to the word "visionary" in contrast with "visual." The records of Wordsworth's visionary hearing range from the formal "soundscapes" which Geoffrey Hartman has analyzed and named in the two long early topographical poems, through the imaginatively dangerous remythologizing of natural music in the interesting and problematic ode "On the Power of Sound." In a section of it, the poet addresses echoes as "Ye Voices, and ye Shadows / And Images of voice—" and these very shadows and images of the exhortation are as much a succedaneum and prop as that of invoking reflections as "echoes of vision" would be a fancy. A British linguistic scholar has put rather well one aspect of this phenomenological commonplace: "sound stands more in need of external support than light, form, or color; hence the greater frequency of the intrusion of outside elements into the description of acoustic phenomena." The "external supports" here are those of metaphor. Shadow, and mirror-image in bronze or water, coexist in antiquity with echoes, and their personifications are parallel myths. But there is no analogue of painting or sculpture for the preservation of aural shades; until the invention of the phonograph, in fact, there is no way of recording sounds of discourse or music save by echoes or parrots. Nor can any dreams and imaginations of the ear save those of human discourse survive the feeble resources of the dreamer's reportage.

Thus, for example, while the afterimage of the daffodils can "flash upon" the inward eye, the immediate presence of the mountain echoes of a reciprocal poem composed two years later are "rebounds our inward ear/ Catches sometimes from afar," a kinetic characterization threatened, rather than elucidated, by the subsequent development of rubber balls. But the cultivation of this "inward ear" is nonetheless an important element in preparing for the representation of consciousness, and it is interesting to observe parallels with, as well as the intersection of, the course of evolving an answerable diction which that element reveals. In 1802 Wordsworth had addressed his brother John as a "*silent* Poet" who "from the solitude / Of the vast sea didst bring a watchful heart / Still couchant, an inevitable ear, / And an eye practised like a blind man's touch." But the openness of the sense of hearing is never the problem: crucial to the economy of the sense is the fact that we cannot close our ears as we do our eyes, and that vision is far more directional than hearing, which is not "To such a tender ball as th'eye confin'd" but, more like feeling, through all parts, at least of the head, "diffus'd." "A man, inasmuch as he has ears," said Emerson, "is accosted by the thunder and the birds." It is more a matter of the availability of appropriate conceptualization for representing the experience of hearing.

—John Hollander, "Wordsworth and the Music of Sound" in *New Perspectives on Coleridge and Wordsworth*, Geoffrey H. Hartman, ed. (New York: Columbia University Press, 1972): pp. 58-59.

[M. H. Abrams, the renowned scholar of romanticism, is Professor of English at Cornell. His writings on the romantic period include *The Mirror and the Lamp: Romantic Theory and the Critical Tradition* (1953) and *Natural Phenomenon: Tradition and Revolution in Romantic Literature* (1971).]

The first critic of Wordsworth's poetry was Wordsworth himself, and in his criticism, as in his poetry, he speaks with two distinct voices. The first voice is that of the "Preface" to *Lyrical Ballads*, in which Wordsworth powerfully applies to his poetry some humanistic values of the European Enlightenment. In his "Preface" the controlling and interrelated norms are the essential, the elementary, the simple, the universal, and the permanent. The great subjects of his poetry, Wordsworth says, are "the essential passions of the heart," "elementary feelings," "the great and simple affections," "the great and universal passions of men," and "characters of which the elements are simple . . . such as exist now, and will probably always exist," as these human qualities interact with "the beautiful and permanent forms of nature." His aim is a poetry written in a "naked and simple" style that is "well adapted to interest mankind permanently." And the poet himself, as "a man speaking to men," both affirms and effects the primal human values: the joy of life, the dignity of life and of its elemental moving force, the pleasure principle, and the primacy of the universal connective, love. The poet "rejoices more than other men in the spirit of life" both within him and without, pays homage "to the grand elementary principle of pleasure, by which he knows, and feels, and lives, and moves," and is "the rock of defense of human nature, carrying everywhere with him relationship and love."

Wordsworth's second critical voice has been far less heeded by his readers. It speaks out in the "Essay, Supplementary to the Preface" of his Poems of 1815, and reiterates in sober prose the claims he had made, years before, in the verse "Prospectus" to *The Recluse* (reprinted in his "Preface" to *The Excursion*) and in the opening and closing passages of *The Prelude:* claims that it is his task to confront and find consolation in human suffering—

whether the "solitary agonies" of rural life or the "fierce confederate storm / Of sorrow" barricaded within the walls of cities—since he is a poet who has been singled out "for holy services" in a secular work of man's "redemption." In his "Essay" of 1815, Wordsworth addresses himself to explain and justify those aspects of novelty and strangeness in his poetry that have evoked from critics "unremitting hostility, . . . slight . . . aversion, . . . contempt." He does so by asserting that he, like every "truly original poet," has qualities that are "peculiarly his own," and in specifying his innovations, he does not now take his operative concepts from eighteenth-century humanism, but imports them from theology; that is, he deliberately adapts to poetry the idiom hitherto used by Christian apologists to justify the radical novelty, absurdities, and paradoxes of the Christian mysteries. For Wordsworth claims in this essay that there are "affinities between religion and poetry," "a community of nature," so that poetry shares the distinctive quality of Christianity, which is to confound "the calculating understanding" by its contradictions:

> For when Christianity, the religion of humility, is founded upon the proudest quality of our nature [the imagination], what can be expected but contradictions?

In the "Essay" of 1815, accordingly, Wordsworth does not represent poetry as elemental and simple, but stresses instead its "contradictions"—that is, its radical paradoxicality, its union of antitheses, its fusion of the sensuous and the transcendent, its violation of the customary, and its reversal of status between the highest and lowest. Poetry, for example, imitates the supreme condition of the Incarnation itself: it is "ethereal and transcendent, yet incapable to sustain her existence without sensuous incarnation." The higher poetry unites the "wisdom of the heart and the grandeur of imagination" and so achieves a "simplicity" that is "Magnificence herself." Wordsworth's own poems manifest "emotions of the pathetic" that are "complex and revolutionary." As for the "sublime"—he is specifically a poet "charged with a new mission to extend its kingdom, and to augment and spread its enjoyments." For as one of the poets who combine the "heroic passions" of pagan antiquity with Christian wisdom, he has produced a new synthesis—an "accord of sublimated humanity." And his chief enterprise as a poet is expressed in a Christian paradox—he must cast his readers down in order to raise them up:

their spirits "are to be humbled and humanized, in order that they may be purified and exalted."

—M. H. Abrams, "Two Roads to Wordsworth" in *Wordsworth: A Collection of Critical Essays*, M. H. Abrams, ed. (Englewood Cliffs, N.J.: Prentice-Hall, 1972): pp. 1–2.

JOHN MAHONEY ON POETIC PLANS WITH COLERIDGE

[John Mahoney is the Thomas F. Rattigan Professor of English at Boston College and specializes in British Enlightenment and Romantic Literature. He has previously published books on Hazlitt, Keats, and Coleridge.]

Suggested here is a key problem associated with the *Lyrical Ballads* of 1798 and 1800—namely, the extent to which the poems are faithful to the ideals set down in the "Preface" concerning people who live close to the land, the language of real men as the proper language of poetry. While we have seen these ideals carried out in the poems we have been discussing, there are others in the *Lyrical Ballads* that strike us by a certain widening of the range of subject matter, with the lyric mode dominating the narrative, with a language still to some extent natural, even conversational, but richer, crisper, more vivid, with an imagery rooted much less in convention and much more in the phenomena of the natural world that surrounded a poet immersed in the sights and sounds of the Lakes. Interestingly, the additions to the original Advertisement and "Preface" are helpful in understanding a somewhat different kind of poem that appears in the 1798 and especially the 1800 editions of the *Lyrical Ballads*, poems that will, it seems, trigger a kind of crossroads situation as Wordsworth contemplates the direction of his work and the course of his career. On the one hand, he remains committed to the poetry of nature—of sea, lake, mountain, sky that surround and, indeed, envelop him; to the people and situations associated with these locales, especially the ordinary, the suffering, the young, the ignored; to a kind of expression that communicates directly and honestly. On the other hand, there is the continuing sense that poetry is the "spontaneous overflow of powerful feelings," that the poet is "a man who, being possessed of more than usual organic sensibility, had also thought long and deeply." There is also that vital modification, later in the "Preface," that poetry, far from glandular response, takes its origin from "emotion recollected in tranquility." And there is the description of the poet as "a man speaking to men: a man, it is true, endowed with more lively sensibility, more enthusiasm and tenderness, who has a greater knowledge of human nature, and a more comprehensive soul, than are supposed to be common among mankind." Such a poet is "a man pleased with his own passions and volitions . . . delighting to contemplate similar volitions and passions as manifested in the goings-on of the Universe, and habitually impelled to create them where he does not find them." More self-conscious, more ready and able to find analogies, images of the inner life within and without, the poet is also a person of great sympathy, with the power to be, more than a mere recorder, an actual participant in what he describes. Mere description and imitation are mechanical; the true poet would "bring his feelings near to those of the persons whose feelings he describes, may, for short spaces of time, perhaps, [would] let himself slip into an entire delusion . . . modifying only the language which is thus suggested to him by a consideration that he describes for a particular purpose, that of giving pleasure."

—John Mahoney, *William Wordsworth: A Poetic Life* (New York: Fordham University Press, 1997): pp. 81–82.

Thematic Analysis of
"The Ruined Cottage"

"The Ruined Cottage" eventually became Book I of Wordsworth's long poem *The Excursion*, published in 1814, but he began work on "The Ruined Cottage" as early as 1797. The poem introduces the character of the Wanderer, who is *The Excursion*'s hero and moral guide. "The Ruined Cottage" is a masterwork of human compassion, the story of a woman named Margaret who is destroyed by a too-strong hope, an inability to accept the losses in her life and move on.

The narrator comes across the old wandering peddler, a dear friend of his, at the site of a deserted, desolate cottage that once belonged to Margaret, her husband Robert, and their two children. The peddler is quintessentially Wordsworthian—old, wise, serene, profound, and inseparable from nature. The Wanderer's childhood is described in the first half of the poem as Wordsworth's vision of an ideal education—shaping and instructing by nature and her rules. He is an exemplary man who insists that he is telling an ordinary story. It is the story of man. The wanderer speaks prophetically, before he begins to tell Margaret's story:

> Thus did he speak. "I see around me here
> Things which you cannot see: we die, my Friend
> Nor we alone, but that which each man loved
> And prized in his peculiar nook of earth
> Dies with him, or is changed; and very soon
>
> Even of the good is no memorial left.

The peddler, a patriarchal figure, expresses a deep sorrow to the narrator. Margaret and he had loved each other like father and daughter:

> The day has been
> When I could never pass this road but she
> Who lived within these walls, when I appeared,
> A daughter's welcome gave me, and I loved her
> As my own child. Oh Sir, the good die first,
> And they whose hearts are dry as summer dust
> Burn to the socket.

Margaret dies young, a victim of her own goodness and particularly of her hope. Hope defines her—hope supported by the memory of her past life with her husband and children. She suffers through bad harvests, a wartime economy, and despair, the things that ultimately drive her husband away. But it is her hope for his return that destroys her. Hope is more terrible than despair, for she holds onto it when she should let it go. Her husband doesn't return. One of her children leaves for a distant farm and the other falls ill and dies. The cottage falls into disrepair and lets in the damp and cold.

> Yet still
> She loved this wretched spot nor would for worlds
> Have parted hence; and still that length of road,
> And this rude bench, one torturing hope endeared,
> Fast rooted at her heart. And here, my friend,
> In sickness she remained; and here she died,
> Last human tenant of these ruined walls.

She dies in nature as does another wanderer in Wordsworth's "The Old Cumberland Beggar." Though Margaret lives in communion with nature, she is not comforted by it as the old Cumberland beggar is. She suffers greatly. After she dies, her cottage disintegrates back into nature.

The poet who is listening to the Wanderer's story is led to the truth as the Wanderer tells the story of the woman who lived in the cottage. The poet reacts:

> The old Man ceased: he saw that I was moved.
> From that low bench rising instinctively,
> I turned aside in weakness, nor had power
> To thank him for the tale which he had told.
> I stood, and leaning o'er the garden gate
> Reviewed that Woman's sufferings; and it seemed
> To comfort me while with a brother's love
> I blessed her in the impotence of grief.

The poet within the poem is moved by this tragic narrative and blesses Margaret, or the memory of Margaret. Both the Wanderer and the poet are enlarged by this story. The tale, the telling, and the listening are all part of Wordsworth's vision of nature's interchange with the mind of man.

The reader is convinced by the end of the poem that Margaret is peaceful because she has been part of the pattern of nature, which is necessarily beneficent.

> She sleeps in the calm earth, and peace is here.
> I well remember those very plumes,
> Those weeds, and the high spear-grass on that wall,
> By mist and silent rain-drops silvered o'er,
> As once I passed, did to my mind convey
> So still an image of tranquility,
> So calm and still, and looked so beautiful
> Amid the uneasy thoughts that filled my mind,
> That what we feel of sorrow and despair
> From ruin and from change, and all the grief
> The passing shows of being leave behind,
> Appeared an idle dream that could not live
> Where meditation was. I turned away
> And walked along my road to happiness.

The poem opens with the recounting of Margaret's death, told at the site of her demise. Before her story begins, the reader knows that her children and then her husband will never return—that her hope is pointless and thus her suffering. The heroine's fate is played out for the reader as another example of nature, this time terrible, but not unnatural and therefore not bad. Margaret is absorbed into her natural surroundings; the cycle is complete. There was no supernatural intervention because nothing could supersede what is nature.

If one removes the treatment of Wordsworth's subjects from the subjects themselves, his world is a dark and despairing place. Despite Wordsworth's vision of the natural world as triumphant, he did not neglect to see the suffering, tortured side of humanity. His own period of despair and crisis had impressed him deeply. The experience led him to a paradoxical discovery—pain and suffering were not unlike happiness and rapture.

Is "The Ruined Cottage" celebratory or tragic? It is both. Margaret was returned to nature—the same nature by which the Wanderer was mothered. The Wanderer tells Margaret's story to the narrator, who is also sustained by nature in a very different way, and they both are enriched by each other, by Margaret, and by nature. It is a process of endless repetition in which the reader is involved once he has apprehended the poem. ❀

Critical Views on
Wordsworth and "The Ruined Cottage"

[Samuel Taylor Coleridge (1772–1834) was a poet and William Wordsworth's closest friend. He and Wordsworth were lifelong creators of poetry, and Coleridge's independent work is of distinction as well as the work he did with Wordsworth. He wrote *Kubla Khan* in 1797 and published *Lyrical Ballads* (created with Wordsworth) in 1798.]

[Wordsworth contains] a meditative pathos, a union of deep and subtle thought with sensibility; a sympathy with man as man; the sympathy indeed of a contemplator, rather than a fellow-sufferer or a co-mate (spectator, *baud particeps*), but of a contemplator, from whose view no difference of rank conceals the sameness of nature; no injuries of wind or weather, of toil, or even of ignorance, wholly disguise the human face divine. The superscription and the image of the Creator still remain legible to him under the dark lines, with which guilt or calamity had cancelled or cross-barred it. Here the man and the poet lose and find themselves in each other, the one as glorified, the latter as substantiated. In this mild and philosophic pathos, Wordsworth appears to me without a compeer. Such he *is*: so he *writes*. ''Tis said that some have died for love' or that most affecting composition, the *Afflictions of Margaret—of—*, which no mother, and if I may judge by my own experience, no parent can read without a tear. Or turn to that genuine lyric, in the former edition, entitled, *The Mad Mother*, of which I cannot refrain from quoting one of the stanzas, for its pathos, and for the fine transition in the two concluding lines of the stanza, so expressive of that deranged state, in which from the increased sensibility the sufferer's attention is abruptly drawn off by every trifle, and in the same instant plucked back again by the one despotic thought, and bringing home with it, by the blending, fusing power of Imagination and Passion, the alien object to which it had been so abruptly diverted no longer an alien but an ally and an inmate:

Suck little babe, oh suck again!
It cools my blood, it cools my brain:
Thy lips, I feel them, baby! they
Draw from my heart the pain away.
Oh! press me with thy little hand;
It loosens something at my chest;
About that tight and deadly band
I feel thy little fingers prest.
The breeze I see is in the trees!
It comes to cool my babe and me.

—S. T. Coleridge, *Biographia Literaria*, 1817.

THOMAS DE QUINCY ON A TRIBUTE TO WORDSWORTH

[Thomas de Quincy (1785–1859) was an English essayist and personal friend to William Wordsworth. The autobiographical *Confessions of an Opium-Eater* (1822) brought him to literary fame. He is also remembered for *On the Knocking at the Gate in Macbeth* and *Autobiographic Sketches* (1853).]

How often (to give an instance or two) must the human heart have felt the case, and yearned for an expression of the case, when there are sorrows which descend far below the region in which tears gather; and yet who has ever given utterance to this feeling until Wordsworth came with his immortal line:

Thoughts that do often lie too deep for tears?

This sentiment, and others that might be adduced (such as 'The child is father to the man'), have even passed into the popular heart, and are often quoted by those who know not whom they are quoting. Magnificent, again, is the sentiment, and yet an echo to one which lurks amongst all hearts, in relation to the frailty of merely human schemes for working good, which so often droop and collapse through the unsteadiness of human energies:

> Foundations must be laid
> In heaven.

How? Foundations laid in realms that are *above?* But *that* is impossible; *that* is at war with elementary physics; foundations must be laid *below*. Yes; and even so the poet throws the mind yet more forcibly on the hyperphysical character—on the grandeur transcending all physics—of those spiritual and shadowy foundations which alone are enduring.

But the great distinction of Wordsworth, and the pledge of his increasing popularity, is the extent of his sympathy with what is *really* permanent in human feelings, and also the depth of this sympathy. Young and Cowper, the two earlier leaders in the province of meditative poetry, are too circumscribed in the range of their sympathies, too narrow, too illiberal, and too exclusive. Both these poets manifest the quality of their strength in the quality of their public reception. Popular in some degree at first, they entered upon the inheritance of their fame almost at once. Far different was the fate of Wordsworth: for in poetry of this class, which appeals to what lies deepest in man, in proportion to the native power of the poet, and his fitness for permanent life, is the strength of resistance in the public taste. Whatever is too original will be hated at the first. It must slowly mould a public for itself; and the resistance of the early thoughtless judgments must be overcome by a counter-resistance to itself in a better audience slowly mustering against the first. Forty and seven years it is since William Wordsworth first appeared as an author. Twenty of those years he was the scoff of the world, and his poetry a byword of scorn. Since then and more than once, senates have rung with acclamations to the echo of his name. Now, at this moment, whilst we are talking about him, he has entered upon his sixty-seventh year. For himself, according to the course of nature, he cannot be far from his setting; but his poetry is only now clearing the clouds that gathered about its rising. Meditative poetry is perhaps that province of literature which will ultimately maintain most power amongst the generations which are coming; but in this department, at least, there is little competition to be apprehended by Wordsworth from anything that has appeared since the death of Shakespeare.

—Thomas de Quincey, *On Wordsworth's Poetry,* 1851.

A. N. WHITEHEAD ON THE REVOLT AGAINST ABSTRACTIONS

[Alfred North Whitehead was the eminent mathematician, philosopher, and essayist who, with Bertrand Russell, wrote *Principia Mathematica* (1910–13), the foundation work of modern symbolic logic. His most widely read books, combining his philosophic ideas with excursions into intellectual history, are *Science and the Modern World* (1926) and *Adventures of Ideas* (1933).]

Wordsworth was passionately absorbed in nature. It has been said of Spinoza, that he was drunk with God. It is equally true that Wordsworth was drunk with nature. But he was a thoughtful, well-read man, with philosophical interests, and sane even to the point of prosiness. In addition, he was a genius. He weakens his evidence by his dislike of science. We all remember his scorn of the poor man whom he somewhat hastily accuses of peeping and botanising on his mother's grave. Passage after passage could be quoted from him, expressing this repulsion. In this respect, his characteristic thought can be summed up in his phrase, "We murder to dissect."

In this latter passage, he discloses the intellectual basis of his criticism of science. He alleges against science its absorption in abstractions. His consistent theme is that the important facts of nature elude the scientific method. It is important therefore to ask, what Wordsworth found in nature that failed to receive expression in science. I ask this question in the interest of science itself; for one main position in these lectures is a protest against the idea that the abstractions of science are irreformable and unalterable. Now it is emphatically not the case that Wordsworth hands over inorganic matter to the mercy of science, and concentrates on the faith that in the living organism there is some element that science cannot analyze. Of course he recognizes, what no one doubts, that in some sense living things are different from lifeless things. But that is not his main point. It is the brooding presence of the hills which haunts him. His theme is nature *in solido*, that is to say, he dwells on that mysterious presence of surrounding things, which imposes itself on any separate element that we set up as an individual for its own sake. He always grasps the whole of nature as involved in the tonality of the particular instance. That is why he laughs with the daffodils, and finds in the primrose "thoughts too deep for tears."

—Alfred N. Whitehead, *Science and the Modern World* (Cambridge: Cambridge University Press, 1926): pp. 22–23.

FREDERICK A. POTTLE ON THE EYE AND THE OBJECT IN WORDSWORTH'S POETRY

[Frederick Pottle is Sterling Professor Emeritus of English at Yale. He is best known as the editor and biographer of James Boswell.]

More than that, a good many of his poems, including several of his finest, either have no basis in personal experience at all, or show autobiography so manipulated that the "subject" corresponds to nothing Wordsworth ever saw with the bodily eye. His extensive critical writings deride the matter-of-fact and speak over and over again of the power of the imagination to modify and create. Yet there is a widespread belief that Wordsworth was Nature's Boswell, in the old erroneous sense which defined Boswell as a man who followed Johnson about with a notebook, taking down his utterances on the spot. Actually, like Boswell, Wordsworth relied on memory, and says so quite explicitly. But then he says other things in which he appears to be vindicating the rightness of his poetry, not on the ground that it is well-imagined, but on the ground that the things described in the poem really did happen in that fashion and in no other. I do not mean merely the notes which he dictated in old age to Miss Fenwick. There is his impassioned defense of *The Leech Gatherer* against the mild and sisterly strictures of Sara Hutchinson, a defense made before the poem was published: "A young Poet in the midst of the happiness of Nature is described as overwhelmed by the thought of the miserable reverses which have befallen the happiest of all men, viz Poets—I think of this till I am so deeply impressed by it, that I consider the manner in which I was rescued from my dejection and despair almost as an interposition of Providence. . . . 'A lonely place, a Pond' 'by which an old man *was*, far from all house or home'—not stood, not sat, but '*was*'—the figure presented in the most naked simplicity possible. . . . I cannot conceive a figure more impressive than that of an old Man like this, the survivor of a Wife and ten children, travelling alone among the mountains and all lonely places, carrying with him his own fortitude, and the necessities which an unjust state of society has entailed upon him. . . . Good God! Such a figure, in such a place, a pious, self-respecting, miserably infirm . . . Old Man telling such a tale!"

Who would believe from reading this that in real life Wordsworth met the old man, not on the lonely moor, but in the highway; that the old man in real life was not demonstrating resolution and independence by gathering leeches under great difficulties, but was begging? In short, that the narrative is from first to last an imaginative construction—the account of an imagined meeting between Wordsworth and the beggar as Wordsworth imagined him to have been before he was finally reduced to beggary?

—Frederick A. Pottle, "The Eye and the Object in the Poetry of Wordsworth," in *The Yale Review* 40 (1950): p. 11.

John Jones on the Baptized Imagination in Wordsworth

[John Jones, a Fellow of Merton College, Oxford, wrote *The Egotistical Sublime* (1954), a study of Wordsworth's poetry; *On Aristotle and Greek Tragedy* (1962); and *John Keats's Dream of Truth* (1969).]

Wordsworth sees Paradise [in the excursion] as a jewelled and holy city, as the New Jerusalem of Revelation. That the city should play this part is at once remarkable, since it has hitherto been very unimportant to him. The city of social and satirical poetry appears scarcely at all, because he was not this kind of poet. The city has no place within the greater landscape: if it has any poetic function, it is the negative one of circumscribing the unmanageable. This not to say that all Wordsworth's poetry of the city is bad: sometimes, as in *The Prelude*'s description of the "anarchy and din" of St. Bartholomew's Fair, the countryman's wide-eyed stare, his fearful amazement, his almost willing fascination, are vividly conveyed. And once or twice, as when he saw London from Westminster Bridge "all bright and glittering" in the dress of early morning, or, in a fine poem which he left unpublished,

> white with winter's purest white, as fair,
> As fresh and spotless as he ever sheds
> On field or mountain,

the city is suddenly transmuted, and one can just understand how he came to see that other that has no need of sun or moon to shine upon it.

Even so, the *Excursion* city is a new thing—Paradise in an exact Christian and literary sense. It would be a tidy thesis that followed Wordsworth's imaginative course from the Garden of Eden in his greater landscape to the New Jerusalem in his late poetry. But it would not be true. The landscape is paradisal only in that difficult sense in which Wordsworth's early poetry is optimistic. Neither is it Christian nor is it the Never Never Land of Classical and Rousseauite myth: it is northern and severe, with a terrible simplicity that the pastoral Wordsworth of Arnold's tradition could not have compassed. And Wordsworth did not see his landscape as he now sees the holy city. Then, the point of his vision was the literalness that enabled him, as he insisted in a hundred different ways, to see things as they are. Now there is a duality which he openly admits. The valley "was visible," yet he did not see it. What he saw—and he italicizes the word so that there shall be no mistake—was "the revealed abode" of the blessed. "Revealed" emphasizes the divine gift of second-sight. We must believe that Wordsworth was in the spirit when he beheld this vision.

Nor does Wordsworth's spiritual eye report anything grey or ghostly: the picture is as brilliant and as substantial as that described in Revelation. This directness of visual appeal owes much to the philosophical innocence that allowed Wordsworth to write about the Kingdom of Heaven unalarmed by the huge difficulties at least as old as Plato's *Parmenides*, that attend belief in a transcendent order of reality. In this *Excursion* passage he is entirely concerned, like Blake, to report what he saw, in the faith that visions justify themselves; and, like Blake, he sees his problem as one of adequate description. Sustained prophetic frenzy is very rare in Wordsworth, but he is clearly attracted to the lunatic state, as to childhood, for its privileged access to the supernatural. A late poem about a woman driven mad by the pain of bereavement ends thus:

> Nor of those maniacs is she one that kiss
> The air or laugh upon a prophetic precipice;
> No, passing through strange sufferings towards the tomb,
> She smiles as if a martyr's crown were won:
> Oft, when light breaks through clouds or waving trees,
> With outspread arms and fallen upon her knees
> The Mother hails in her descending Son
> An Angel, and in earthly ecstasies
> Her own angelic glory seems begun.

—John Jones, "Wordsworth: The Baptized Imagination" in *The Egotistical Sublime: A History of Wordsworth's Imagination* (London: Chatto and Windus Ltd., 1954): pp. 189–190.

NEIL HERTZ ON WORDSWORTH AND THE TEARS OF ADAM

[Neil Hertz teaches English at Cornell. He has written various critical essays and is at work on a study of the Miltonic tradition through Wordsworth.]

"The Ruined Cottage" was more or less completed in 1798, not long after Wordsworth composed "A Night-Piece," but it was not immediately published. It was put aside for a few years, taken up and revised during the winter of 1801–02, then finally printed as the first book of *The Excursion* in 1814. There it serves as an introduction to the character Wordsworth calls "the Wanderer," who functions as the poet's hero and spokesman throughout that long work. In its final form, "The Ruined Cottage" begins with the poet moving "across a bare wide Common," toward a prearranged meeting with the Wanderer, a rendezvous set in a shady grove surrounding an abandoned and dilapidated cottage. Wordsworth comes in sight of the grove, but postpones his account of their meeting until he has described at length how the Wanderer had come to be as he is, an exemplary Wordsworthian man, aged, wisely passive, profoundly and serenely in touch with Nature. The description of the Wanderer's childhood could have been composed for the opening books of *The Prelude,* but Wordsworth avoids insisting on his likeness to the older man. Rather he admiringly sets the Wanderer off at a distance, in a realm of calm self-possession that the poet himself has yet to attain. This distancing provides Wordsworth with a principle of dramatic structure for the rest of the poem, which falls quite naturally into two roughly equal sections. The first describes the Wanderer's education, a model of the gentle and molding power of Nature; the second half of the poem obliquely echoes this process, for it is concerned with what is really an incident in the poet's education, although this time it is not Nature but the Wanderer's words that exercise the benign influence. Like Adam listening to Michael, Wordsworth is gradually led toward the truth, and toward the appropriate response to the truth, as he listens to the Wanderer tell a sad story, the history of the last occupants of the now-ruined cottage.

Characteristically, the Wanderer insists that what he is telling is only "a common tale, / An ordinary sorrow of man's life," but the accents in which he begins his story mark his intention as prophetic:

> Thus did he speak. "I see around me here
> Things which you cannot see: we die, my Friend,
> Nor we alone, but that which each man loved
> And prized in his peculiar nook of earth
> Dies with him, or is changed; and very soon
> Even of the good is no memorial left.

And that is the burden of the story which follows. A family disintegrates; the wife, Margaret, abandoned by her husband, gradually loses hope of his return, allows one of her children to leave her for a distant farm, the other to fall ill and die. She herself finally dies, and her cottage and its garden are now to be seen caught in the slow process of wasting back into the landscape. Like Milton's story of the Flood, the story of Margaret may be taken as an object lesson: the dead child, the overgrown garden, the ruined cottage speak of the same losses that Adam is made to feel as he learns that the Flood will sweep away his descendants and his dwelling-place; and the play of Wordsworth's curiosity and grief against the wiser but not entirely impassive understanding of the Wanderer recapitulates the dialogue of Adam and the Archangel. There is even a Wordsworthian analogue of the redemptive process, for it is suggested that Nature herself, the Nature that ministered to the Wanderer as a child, is providentially overseeing this episode in human history. But it is chiefly in the telling of the tale, in the rehearsal in words of the truth of loss, that the poem asserts a saving continuity; the pathos of Margaret's history is given additional depth and poignancy because it comes to us as a story within a story, and, just as in Paradise Lost, a chain of mediations is established that brings the reader into the continuum, into the repetitive process by which reality is turned into truth.

These structural and thematic resemblances would, in themselves, make us suspect that Wordsworth had meditated on Milton's story of the Flood. But they also can tell us more than that, for they point beyond the similarities of these particular texts toward a clue to Milton's influence on Wordsworth, and possibly to the general nature of literary influence. In this particular case, influence is best understood not by picking up the echoes of specific bits of Milton's language or the reappearance of Miltonic themes, but by noticing the interrelation of theme and structure, of the theme of loss and the structure of narrative. The loss of human continuities is the burden of ordinary historical time; the creation of another order of time, in which that loss is confronted and acknowledged, is the achievement of narrative. Taken singly, both the poetry of the Flood and "The Ruined Cottage" embody these truths; taken together, they exemplify the kind of continuity with which each is concerned. For the encounter of poet with poet is analogous to that of Michael with Adam, or of Milton with Adam, or of Wordsworth with the Wanderer.

—Neil Hertz, "Wordsworth and the Tears of Adam" in *Studies in Romanticism* 7 (1967): pp. 120–121.

JONATHAN WORDSWORTH ON "THE RUINED COTTAGE" AS TRAGIC NARRATIVE

[Jonathan Wordsworth, a descendant of the poet's brother Christopher, is the University Lecturer in Romantic Studies at Oxford, Fellow of St. Catherine's College, and Chairman of the Wordsworth Trust, Grasmere. He is the author of *The Music of Humanity: A Critical Study of*

"The Ruined Cottage" as a whole is remarkable for the extent to which Wordsworth has visualized the movements and positions of his characters. Again and again a brief reference to the setting intensifies one's response:

> Margaret looked at me
> A little while, then turned her head away
> Speechless, and *sitting down upon a chair*
> Wept bitterly.

>   "I perceive
> You look at me, and you have cause. . . . "

The last part of Margaret's story particularly depends on this technique. Up to this point Wordsworth has recorded the stages of her decline, but now his precise time-sequence is abandoned, and he talks instead of "*the* warm summer," "*the* long winter." Five tedious years are evoked in a series of moving individual scenes: Margaret on her bench, her eye

> busy in the distance, shaping things
> Which made her heart beat quick.

Margaret spinning hemp, but stopping to ask soldiers and crippled sailors about Robert; Margaret standing to open the gate for horsemen so that she may ask "the same sad question"—if she dares; Margaret, "Last human tenant" of walls already ruined. She dies, still hoping, of sickness brought on by the decay of her cottage. On a conscious level she has "no wish to live," and though kept alive by torturing hope she cannot keep up the routine of survival, symbolized in Robert's closing up of chinks "At the first nippings of October frost." There is no question of despair, but hope is no longer the resilient optimism which enabled her to take up Robert's tools at the end of the Pedlar's first visit:

> And so she lived
> Through the long winter, reckless and alone,
> Till this reft house, by frost, and thaw, and rain,
> Was sapped; and when she slept, the nightly damps
> Did chill her breast, and in the stormy day

Her tattered clothes were ruffled by the wind
Even at the side of her own fire. Yet still
She loved this wretched spot, nor would for worlds
Have parted hence; and still that length of road
And this rude bench, one torturing hope endeared,
Fast rooted at her heart. And here, my friend,
In sickness she remained; and here she died,
Last human tenant of these ruined walls.

—Jonathan Wordsworth, *The Music of Humanity: A Critical Study of Wordsworth's "Ruined Cottage"* (London: Thomas Nelson and Sons, 1969): pp. 124–125.

THOMAS MCFARLAND ON THE WORDSWORTHIAN RIGIDITY

[Thomas McFarland is Professor of English at Princeton University. He is widely known for his books on Coleridge and on Shakespeare, as well as for his *Romanticism and the Forms of Ruin*.]

It was as though Wordsworth's psychic muscles were constantly tensed. The initial life-giving radiance—the sense that "Heaven lies about us in our infancy"—was left further and further behind as the years went by. Though the growing boy beheld "the light, and whence it flows," the "Youth" daily traveled "farther from the east"; at length "the Man" perceived it "die away,/ And fade into the light of common day." The course of existence therefore offered the prospect not of an accession but a deprivation of being: "I see by glimpse now; when age comes on / May scarcely see at all"; "Life's autumn past, I stand on winter's verge; / And daily lose what I desire to keep." In this respect Wordsworth's life of eighty years, in itself an anomaly among ruptured Romantic existences, was a cruel irony, a long day's dying to augment his pain. What he always wanted was to experience unchangingly the joy he had felt as a child—"Stability without regret or fear; / That hath been, is, and shall be evermore." Thus the Solitary, commenting on the happiness of a "cottage boy," says "Far happiest . . . / If, such as now he is, he might remain."

But into the longing for eternal and blessèd childhood obtruded the iron claims of ravaging time:

> ... a thought arose
> Of life continuous, Being unimpaired;
> That hath been, is, and where it was and is
> There shall endure,—existence unexposed
> To the blind walk of mortal accident;
> From diminution safe and weakening age;
> While man grows old, and dwindles, and decays;
> And countless generations of mankind
> Depart; and leave no vestige where they trod.

We recognize the lines as not merely the poetic precursor of Keats's "Ode to a Nightingale" but also as an index for the peculiarly tragic sense of Wordsworth's life. The cheerfulness of the egotistical sublime was an attempt to maintain the thought of "life continuous, Being unimpaired." The cost of such continual straining against the true situation of "mortal accident," "diminution," and "weakening age" was the Wordsworthian rigidity: the psychic muscles were always tensed. A trifling comment from the last decade of Wordsworth's life reveals, perhaps better than larger evidence, Wordsworth's own haunted sense of this fact:

> Nothing however said or done to me for some time has in relation to myself given me so much pleasure as a casual word of Anna's that the expression of my face was ever varying. I had begun to fear that it had lately been much otherwise.

> —Thomas McFarland, "The Wordsworthian Rigidity" in *Romanticism and the Forms of Ruin: Wordsworth, Coleridge, and the Modalities of Fragmentation* (Princeton, N.J.: Princeton University Press, 1981): p. 152.

Works by
William Wordsworth

The standard collected edition of Wordsworth's poems remains the five-volume edition edited by Ernest de Selincourt: *The Poetical Works of William Wordsworth*, 5 vols., Oxford University Press, 1952. There is, however, a series of books emerging to compete with the de Selincourt edition, which offers the various versions of Wordsworth's poems. This is the *Cornell Wordsworth* series, general editor Stephen Parish, Ithaca: Cornell University Press. This was begun in 1975 and is an ongoing project.

The standard edition of Wordsworth's prose is the three-volume set published by Oxford: *The Prose Works of William Wordsworth*, ed. W. J. B. Owen and Jane Worthington Smyser, 3 vols., Oxford University Press, 1974.

Works about
William Wordsworth

Abrams, Meyer Howard, ed. *Wordsworth: A Collection of Critical Essays.* Englewood Cliffs, NJ: Prentice-Hall, 1972.

Averill, James H. *Wordsworth and the Poetry of Human Suffering.* Ithaca: Cornell University Press, 1980.

Baker, Jeffrey. *Time and Mind in Wordsworth's Poetry.* Detroit, MI.: Wayne State University Press, 1980.

Beer, John Bernard. *Wordsworth and the Human Heart.* New York: Columbia University Press, 1978.

Bialostosky, Don H. *Making Tales: The Poetics of Wordsworth's Narrative Experiments.* Chicago: The University of Chicago Press, 1984.

Bloom, Harold. *The Visionary Company: A Reading of Romantic Poetry.* Ithaca: Cornell University Press, 1971.

Brett, R. L., and Jones, A. R., eds. *Lyrical Ballads, 1798 and 1800.* London: Methuen, 1978.

Butler, James, ed. *The Ruined Cottage and The Pedlar.* Ithaca: Cornell University Press, 1979.

Byatt, Antonia Susan. *Wordsworth and Coleridge in Their Time.* London: Nelson, 1970.

Coleridge, Samuel Taylor. *Biographia Literaria.* Eds. James Engell and W. Jackson Bate. 2 vols. Princeton: Princeton University Press, 1983.

_____. *Coleridge's Poems and Prose.* Selected by Kathleen Raine. London: Penguin, 1957.

_____. *Collected Letters of Samuel Taylor Coleridge.* Ed. Earl Leslie Griggs. 6 vols. Oxford: Oxford University Press, 1912.

Curtis, Jared. *The Fenwick Notes of William Wordsworth.* London: Bristol Classical Press, 1993.

Davies, Hunter. *William Wordsworth, A Biography.* London: Weidenfield and Nicolson, 1980.

De Selincourt, Ernest. *The Early Wordsworth.* The English Association Presidential Address, November 1936. Oxford: Oxford University Press, 1936.

Devlin, David Douglas. *Wordsworth and the Poetry of Epitaphs*. London: Macmillan Press, 1980.

_____. *Wordsworth and the Art of Prose*. London: Macmillan Press, 1983.

Ferguson, Frances. *Wordsworth: Language as Counter-Spirit*. New Haven: Yale University Press, 1977.

Gérard, Albert S. *English Romantic Poetry: Ethos, Structure, and Symbol in Coleridge, Wordsworth, Shelley, and Keats*. Berkeley: University of California Press, 1968.

Gill, Stephen, ed. *The Salisbury Plain Poems of William Wordsworth*. Ithaca: Cornell University Press, 1975.

_____, ed. *William Wordsworth*. New York: Oxford University Press, 1984.

_____. *Wordsworth: A Life*. Oxford: Clarendon, 1989.

Grob, Alan. *The Philosophic Mind: A Study of Wordsworth's Poetry and Thought, 1797-1805*. Columbus: Ohio University Press, 1973.

Halliday, F. E. *Wordsworth and His World*. London: Thames and Hudson, 1970.

Hartman, Geoffrey. *Wordsworth's Poetry*. New Haven: Yale University Press, 1971.

_____, ed. *New Perspectives on Coleridge and Wordsworth*. New York: Columbia University Press, 1972.

Havens, Raymond Dexter. *The Mind of a Poet*. Baltimore: Johns Hopkins University Press, 1941

Hayden, John O., ed. *The Poems of William Wordsworth*. New Haven: Yale University Press, 1981.

Heath, William. *Wordsworth and Coleridge: A Study of Their Literary Relations in 1801–1802*. New York: Oxford University Press, 1970.

Heffernan, James A. W. *William Wordsworth's Theory of Poetry: The Transforming Imagination*. Ithaca: Cornell University Press, 1969.

Hodgson, John A. *Wordsworth's Philosophical Poetry 1797–1814*. Lincoln: University of Nebraska Press, 1980.

Jackson, Wallace. *The Probable and The Marvelous: Blake, Wordsworth, and the 18th Century Critical Tradition*. Athens: University of Georgia Press, 1978.

Jacobus, Mary. *Tradition and Experiment in Wordsworth's Lyrical Ballads (1798)*. Oxford: Clarendon Press, 1976.

Jaye, Michael C., Jonathan Wordsworth, and Robert Woof. *William Wordsworth and the Age of English Romanticism*. London: Rutgers University Press, 1987.

Johnson, Lee M. *Wordsworth's Metaphysical Verse: Geometry, Nature, and Form*. Toronto: University of Toronto Press, 1982.

Johnston, Kenneth R. *Wordsworth and* The Recluse. New Haven: Yale University Press, 1984.

Jones, Henry John Franklin. *The Egotistical Sublime: A History of Wordsworth's Imagination*. London: Chatto and Windus, 1954.

King, Alexander. *Wordsworth and the Artist's Vision*. London: Athlone Publishers, 1966.

Mahoney, John L. *William Wordsworth: A Poetic Life*. New York: Fordham University Press, 1997.

McConnel, Frank D. *The Confessional Imagination: A Reading of Wordsworth's Prelude*. Baltimore: Johns Hopkins University Press, 1974.

McFarland, Thomas. *Romanticism and the Forms of Ruin: Wordsworth, Coleridge, and the Modalities of Fragmentation*. Princeton: Princeton University Press, 1981.

Moorman, Mary. *William Wordsworth: A Biography*. Vol. I. *The Early Years:1770–1803*. Oxford: Clarendon, 1957; Vol. II. *The Later Years: 1803–1850*. Oxford: Clarendon, 1965.

Murray, Roger. *Wordsworth's Style, Figures, and Themes in the Lyrical Ballads of 1800*. Lincoln: University of Nebraska Press, 1967.

Onorato, Richard. *The Character of the Poet: Wordsworth in "The Prelude."* Princeton: Princeton University Press, 1971.

Owen, W. J. B., ed. *Wordsworth's Literary Criticism*. London: Routledge and Kegan Paul, 1974.

Owen, W. J. B., and Smyser, Jayne Worthington, eds. *The Prose Works of William Wordsworth*. Oxford: Clarendon Press, 1974.

Parrish, Stephen Maxfield. *The Art of the Lyrical Ballads*. Cambridge: Harvard University Press, 1973.

_____, ed. *The Prelude, 1798–1799*. Ithaca: Cornell University Press, 1977.

Perkins, David. *The Quest for Permanence: The Symbolism of Wordsworth, Shelley, and Keats*. Cambridge: Harvard University Press, 1959.

_____. *Wordsworth and the Poetry of Sincerity*. Cambridge: Belknap Press, 1964.

Pirie, David. *William Wordsworth: The Poetry of Grandeur and of Tenderness*. London: Methuen, 1982.

Reed, Mark L. *Wordsworth: The Chronology of the Middle Years, 1800–1815*. Cambridge: Harvard University Press, 1975.

Reguerio, Helen. *The Limits of Imagination: Wordsworth, Yeats, and Stevens*. Ithaca: Cornell University Press, 1976.

Rehder, Robert. *Wordsworth and the Beginnings of Modern Poetry*. Totowa, NJ: Barnes and Noble, 1981.

Roper, Derek, ed. *Lyrical Ballads, 1805*. London: Collins, 1968.

Sheats, Paul D., ed. *The Poetical Works of Wordsworth*. Boston: Houghton Mifflin, 1982.

Sherry, Charles. *Wordsworth's Poetry of the Imagination*. Oxford: Clarendon Press, 1980.

Simpson, David. *Wordsworth and the Figurings of the Real*. London: Macmillan, 1982.

Watson, J. R. *Wordsworth's Vital Soul: The Sacred and the Profane in Wordsworth's Poetry*. London: Macmillan, 1982.

Index of
Themes and Ideas

"ANIMAL TRANQUILITY AND DECAY," 23

DESCRIPTIVE SKETCHES, 11

ECCLESIASTICAL SONNETS, THE, 13

EVENING WALK, AN, 11

EXCURSION, THE, 45, 53; city and, 62; human suffering and, 49–50

"HOME AT GRASMERE," 32–33

"IDIOT BOY, THE," 22, 37

"IMMORTALITY ODE," 22

"INCIPIENT MADNESS," 34

LEECH GATHERER, THE, 60–61

LYRICAL BALLADS, 35–52; Advertisement to, 3, 35, 40–41, 44, 51; common people in, 51; conversational style of, 35; dramatic mono-logue and, 44–45; familiarity of, 42–43; feelings and, 51–52; imagina-tion in, 35, 36, 44–45; nature in, 35, 36, 39–40, 41, 51; originality of, 42, 43; Preface to, 36–37, 38, 49, 51, 52; purpose of, 35; sentiment of "Being" and, 22; thematic analysis of, 35–37

"MAD MOTHER," 34

"NIGHT-PIECE, THE," 63

"OLD CUMBERLAND BEGGAR, THE," 54

PETER BELL, 13

POEMS IN TWO VOLUMES, 13

PRELUDE, THE, 10, 15–34, 45; as autobiographical, 114; boy in, 24; central question of, 17; city and, 61; critical views on, 20–34; despair in, 17–18; factual validity of, 27; growth of poet's own mind and, 9, 15; heart associated with mother and death in, 29–30; human suffering and, 49–50; imagination in, 24–25, 26, 29, 30–32; landscapes of, 30; memory in, 18–19, 27; mother-infant relationship in, 28–29; nature and, 16, 17, 19, 23–25, 28–30, 38; *Prelude* of 1805 and, 15, 16; *Prelude* of 1850 and, 15, 16; as revolution in poetry, 18; sentiment of "Being" in, 21–22; "spots of time" in, 17, 25–26, 30; textual history of, 15; thematic analysis of, 15–19; two consciousnesses in, 18, 26–28; two-part *Prelude* of 1799 and, 15–16, 25–26; union between mind and nature and, 18

RECLUSE, THE, 45; "Home at Grasmere and," 32–33; human suffering and, 49–50; *The Prelude* as preparatory poem for, 15, 27; union between nature and mind and, 18

RIVER DUDDON, 13

"RUINED COTTAGE, THE," 10, 53–68; Adam and, 64–65; critical views on, 56–68; human suffering in, 55, 56; Margaret in, 9, 21, 53–55, 56, 64, 65, 66; Milton and, 64, 65; narrator in, 53, 55; nature in, 53, 54–55, 56, 63–64; thematic analysis of, 53–55; as tragic narrative, 65–67; union between mind and nature in, 54–55; Wanderer in, 21, 53, 54, 55, 63–64, 65

"THORN, THE," 44–45

"TINTERN ABBEY," 10, 35, 41–42; Goody Blake in, 41; critical views on, 39–52; Dorothy and, 38; Harry Gill in, 41; memory in, 38; nature and, 29, 37–38, 41–42, 45–47; sentiment of "Being" and, 22; thematic analysis of, 37–38; union between mind and nature in, 45–47

"WE ARE SEVEN," 22

WORDSWORTH, WILLIAM: abstraction of science and, 59; autobiographical nature of poetry, 60; biography of, 11–14, 32–34; Blake and, 62; Coleridge and, 12, 13, 15, 22, 32, 33, 35, 36, 42, 43, 45, 51–52, 56–57; consolation from poetry of, 9–10; current criticism of, 10; emotional range and intensity of, 10; Enlightenment and, 49, 60; feelings and, 51–52, 57–58; Godwin and, 37; imagination and, 50, 60–63; influence of, 9; Keats and, 24, 46, 68; meditative poetry and, 58; memory and, 60–61; Milton and, 16; nature and, 16, 17, 21, 23–25, 39, 49, 50, 58, 59–60; old men and, 23, 44, 60–61, 63; originality of, 9–10, 20–21, 40, 58; on poetry, 36–37, 38, 40–41, 42, 49–52; religion and, 50–51, 60–63; sentiment of "Being" and, 21–23; Shelley and, 46; sound and, 47–48